WHO KILLED AUNG SAN?

WHO KILLED AUNG SAN?

Kin Oung

White Lotus
Bangkok   Cheney

In Memory of
James Leander Nichols
1931–22 June 1996

Acting consul for Denmark, Finland and Norway.
Correspondent for Switzerland in **Burma.**
Mr. Nichols was acting on behalf of these countries without official
recognition by the **SLORC regime**.
He was convicted and sentenced to 3 years in prison for the
unauthorized possession of 2 fax machines and 7 telephones.
He died in Insein prison in **Rangoon**.

First edition 1993
Second expanded edition 1996

White Lotus Co., Ltd.
G.P.O. Box 1141
Bangkok 10501
Thailand

Printed in Thailand

Typeset by COMSET Limited Partnership

ISBN 974-8496-68-6   (White Lotus Co., Ltd.; Bangkok)
ISBN 1-879155-70-2   (White Lotus Co., Ltd.; Cheney)

This is the sorrowful story,
told as the twilight fails.
And the monkeys walk together,
holding their neighbours' tails.

Rudyard Kipling: *The Legends of Evil*

Contents

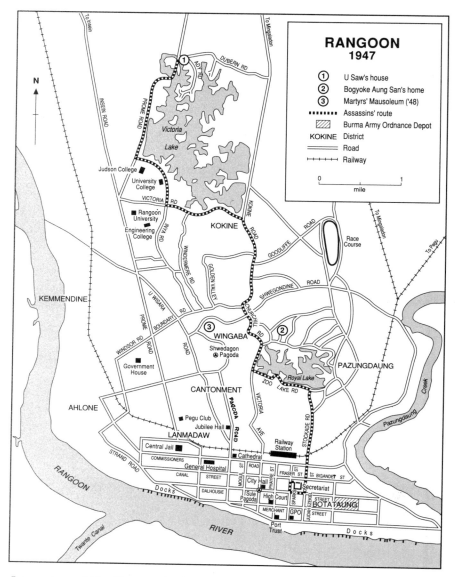

By courtesy of The Cartography Unit Research School of Pacific and Asian Studies;
Australian National University; Canberra, Australia.

Foreword

When I arrived in Rangoon in 1951 to open the first Australian diplomatic mission to Burma the country was still suffering from the shock of the assassination of the leader who had brought the country through the Japanese occupation and had won self-government from the British. U Aung San and most of his colleagues were killed by machine-gun fire at a cabinet meeting on 19 July 1947. This meant the loss not only of the country's most charismatic political figure and leader of the Thirty Comrades but also of six of the brilliant councillors who had been expected to play the leading role in Burma's transition from a British colony to an independent nation.

Although U Saw and the five who carried out the killings were later tried and found guilty there was much that remained mysterious about the assassination. U Kin Oung's book gives a fascinating account of his patient attempts over the years to unravel the full story. He throws a revealing light on British imperial rule in Burma in its last days and provides a vivid insight into the motives and personalities of the main protagonists of this turbulent period.

If Aung San and his six colleagues had not been murdered the subsequent history of Burma would have been very different. At the end of the war the prospects for the establishment of a free and independent nation were good. Compared with other parts of Asia the standard of living was high, and the Irrawaddy river and its delta provided abundant crops of rice and other agricultural products. It also had small but promising sources of oil and other minerals; and its peoples had one of the highest levels of literacy in the region.

World War II and its aftermath had brought great sufferings to the people. The country had been a battleground between British, Chinese and Japanese armies. At the end of the war it was plunged into civil strife, the seeds of which had been sown during the colonial era. Like so many other imperialists the British had governed by the principle of "divide and rule", and had armed and trained non-Burman groups to provide the military forces with which it controlled the country. Not unnaturally this had been resented by the Burmans and as the final withdrawal of the British approached conflict broke out between them and the Karens, the Kachins, and the Shans.

Despite the cruel loss of its experienced leaders the country had by 1950 begun to establish democratic forms of government, and reconciliation was being sought with the dissident communities. It had already been achieved with the Shans, who had accepted a prominent role in the central government. Work had also begun on reconstructing the economy and Burma was resuming its place as a supplier of top-quality rice to the rest of the region. Plans were even being made to reopen to tourists the beautiful countryside and the splendid historical monuments of Pagan and other centres of Burmese civilisation.

All these achievements were nullified in 1962, when General Ne Win over-threw the elected government and installed a military dictatorship. One of the reasons why he was able to do so was undoubtedly the loss suffered by the civilian leadership through the assassinations of 1947. Another was the creation of a military caste as a result of the civil war. Once generals get a taste for power they find it hard to give it up. It gives them great personal privileges and a sense of superiority over ordinary mortals. They are, however, mostly uneducated in any real sense, and have no understanding of the complexities of government in the modern world. They therefore take the easy way—which is to cut the country off from the outside world and stifle the wishes of the people for democratic forms of government.

The rights of the Burmese people will not, however, always be denied. Aung San's daughter, Aung San Suu Kyi, is the leader of the democratic movement in the country and although she is at the time of writing held under house arrest by the military dictators she provides a focus for the people's aspirations for freedom. She has strong support throughout the world in her struggle, not only from the Burmese who have gone into exile but from all those who oppose the evils of military dictatorship and the abuse of human rights that it inevitably entails.

In Australia one of the most active fighters for the rights of the people of Burma is Kin Oung, the author of this book. He was chairman of the Committee for Restoration of Democracy in Burma (Australia) from 1988 to 1992, and vice chairman of the international committee. He was the representative in Australia of the government in exile, the National Coalition Government of the Union of Burma, in 1991.

Kin Oung and his wife, Patricia, belong to families of high distinction in Burmese history. He is the son of the late General Tun Hla Oung, and his wife's father was Thaung Sein, a member of the Indian Civil Service who was after independence Justice of the High Court of Burma. Kin Oung served with the Burma Independence Army and the Burma Navy, and after the war had a distinguished career in the shipping industry. He and his wife lived for 12 years in the United States, before settling in Canberra in 1983.

The author's personal knowledge of the events and the participants in the assassination of Aung San, and his researches into the secret documents held in the British archives, mean that he is exceptionally qualified to tell the story of this critical period in the history of modern Burma. Some mysteries remain—it is still hard to understand what motivated U Saw to perpetrate such cruel and senseless murders—but this book provides indispensable background to scholars who seek insight into Burma in the post-war period and into its subsequent history.

In his book *Breakthrough in Burma* Dr. Ba Maw, who was head of state during the Japanese occupation, insisted that the truth about Burma could never be known until the Burmese themselves told it. He said that the Burmese had not yet written their history of the war and post-war years and nothing that happened in Burma could be really understood until those in a position to know gave their own account. Kin Oung's book makes an invaluable contribution to providing the kind of insight into crucial events of the period for which Dr. Ba Maw called.

Malcolm Booker
Canberra, November 1992

Preface

My late father-in-law, Justice Thaung Sein, used to come to visit us in Canberra from his home in Melbourne about once a year until his death in July 1989. An octogenarian with a lucid mind, he would reminisce to us about various stages in his career, which often reflected important events in modern Burmese history. He had been a member of the élite Indian Civil Service (ICS), serving concurrently as Judicial Secretary and Inspector General of Prisons in 1947. After Burma's independence from Britain in 1948, he was appointed Judge of the High Court and later also headed the Nationalisation and Electoral Appeal Commissions.

One of his favourite anecdotes concerned my late father, Maj.-Gen. Tun Hla Oung, who was the Deputy Inspector General of the Criminal Investigation Department and a member of the prestigious Imperial Police in the late 1940s. When U Saw was incarcerated in Insein Jail, accused of having masterminded the assassination of Bogyoke Aung San and his ministers on 19 July 1947, Maj.-Gen. Tun Hla Oung and Justice Thaung Sein were made jointly responsible for his security. They drove together from Rangoon to Insein Jail almost every day. Their car had to pass through a number of strict check-points, some of them manned by irregular militiamen of the two factions of the People's Volunteer Organisation (PVO), whose loyalties were always dubious. One evening in late 1947, the vehicle carrying my father and my father-in-law was gruffly called to a halt at a barrier. Men in a motley array of uniforms came running out at them with rifles at the ready. My father, who was at the wheel, alighted. Identifying himself and his companion, he knocked the rifle out of the hands of the leader of the armed men, climbed back into the car, and drove away.

The recounting of that encounter triggered my interest in the political drama of that time. I was fascinated by the mix of Imperial law and indigenous lawlessness, involving the private armies of politicians and the various, often conflicting interests they served—but the notorious Galon U Saw, who had also had his band of armed followers, called the *Galon Tat* ("the Garuda Force") after a powerful bird in Hindu mythology, intrigued me most of all.

My two young sons, Kin Oo Oung and Tun Hla Oung Jr, often joined me in coaxing Grandpa to continue his story-telling. We would all listen entranced as he told us about U Saw's mysterious exchange of coded letters with his accomplices over the murder of our national leaders. There was "the sinister ghost that limped", "bananas served green", the love of "lemonade", why "the lake had no fish", and the mystery of "the tall man". I began to suspect that the assassination of Aung San had not been the work of U Saw and his men alone and that it might have involved more people who were never brought to justice.

I felt I had to write down my father-in-law's words so that others would know more about the story. My scattered notes grew into essays, which he would read and approve. Gradually my writings expanded as I supplemented his reminiscences with my own and further reading. I too had lived through that tumultuous era as a young naval officer stationed at the base across the road from the Secretariat, where the assassinations had taken place.

Another source of inspiration was my uncle U Shwe Baw, ICS and Secretary of the Executive Council—the pre-independence cabinet—who was seated on the left of Aung San on that fateful day in July 1947. He miraculously escaped unscathed to tell me his eye-witness account of the tragedy.

This book may raise more questions than it answers, but it has been my intention to sort out some of the mystery surrounding Aung San's assassination and to initiate a new, more thorough look at an event that more than any other has shaped the destiny of our country. It is my conviction, and the firm belief of the vast majority of my countrymen, that many of Burma's subsequent misfortunes could have been avoided had Aung San lived. For this reason alone it is important to analyse the event—and the legacy of avarice and violence that has characterised the political scene in Burma ever since the founder of our new republic was killed 45 years ago.

This book is dedicated to the people who have resisted this legacy and are fighting bravely for the cause of freedom, democracy, and harmony in Burma.

Kin Oung
Canberra, November 1992

Dramatis Personae[1]

The Martyrs

Bogyoke Aung San, alias Bo Teza, 32. The paramount leader of the Burmese nationalist movement. Deputy Chairman of the Executive Council, or, in effect, Prime Minister in the pre-independence cabinet. Also Councillor for Defence and External Affairs. Received 13 bullet wounds and died on the spot.

Deedok U Ba Choe, 54. Writer, journalist, and editor of the *Deedok* magazine. Councillor for Information. Despite his age and the five bullets he took, one in the brain, he survived in Rangoon General Hospital until the afternoon.

Thakin Mya, 49. The elder statesman among the young leaders. Councillor for Finance. Shot through the lungs and died on the spot.

U Abdul Razak, 49. A Muslim leader from Mandalay. Councillor for Education and National Planning. Received six wounds and died on the spot.

U Ba Win, 46. Aung San's elder brother. Councillor for Commerce and Supplies. Received eight bullet wounds and died on the spot.

Mahn Ba Khaing, 43. A Karen from Henzada who had participated in the resistance during the Japanese occupation. Councillor for Industry and Labour. Hit by 15 bullets, some through the heart. Died on the spot.

Sao Sam Htun, 40. The *sawbwa* of the Shan state of Möng Pawn. Councillor for Frontier Areas. Received two wounds in the head and died in Rangoon General Hospital at noon on the 20th.

U Ohn Maung, 34. Deputy Secretary in the Department of Transport and Communications. Came to deliver a report when he was cut down by the assassins' bullets. Killed on the spot.

Ko Htwe, 18. U Razak's bodyguard. A Muslim boy from Taungbyin Theikpanyat near Mandalay. On hearing the gunfire in the meeting room, he rushed out of a nearby office and was shot by the retreating assassins. Received four wounds and died in hospital.

The Assassins

U Saw. Born in 1900 in Tharrawaddy. Alleged ringleader. Veteran right-wing politician and Aung San's main rival. Founder of the *Sun* newspaper and leader of the *Myochit* ("Patriots") Party. Prime Minister, September 1940–January 1942. Interned in Uganda, 1942–6. Repudiated the January 1947 Aung San–Attlee agreement. Arrested on 19 July 1947 for the murder of Aung San and his Executive Council colleagues. Convicted as charged and hanged on 8 May 1948.

Maung Soe. Gunman. Sentenced to death. Executed in May 1948.

Thet Hnin. Gunman. Sentenced to death. Executed in May 1948.

Maung Sein. Gunman. Sentenced to death. Executed in May 1948.

Yan Gyi Aung. At 18, the youngest of the gunmen. Sentenced to death. Executed in May 1948.

Thu Kha. Driver of the jeep that took the assassins to the Secretariat. Given the death sentence, which was later reduced to 20 years' imprisonment.

Khin Maung Yin. Accomplice. Given the death sentence, which was later reduced to 20 years' imprisonment.

Maung Ni. Accomplice. Given the death sentence, which was later reduced to 20 years' imprisonment.

Hmon Gyi. Accomplice. Sentenced to death. Executed in May 1948.

Ba Nyunt. U Saw's chief henchman. Assigned to kill U Nu. Turned Approver to give King's evidence. Granted conditional pardon. Sentenced to ten years and six months' rigorous imprisonment.

The Law

Justice Kyaw Myint. Born in 1898. Barrister and Advocate of the High Court (from 1946). President of the Special Tribunal that tried U Saw. Tin Tut's brother. After independence, Judge of the Supreme Court.

U Aung Tha Gyaw. Senior Sessions Judge. Member of the Special Tribunal that tried U Saw. After independence, Judge of the High Court, then Judge of the Supreme Court.

U Si Bu. Senior Sessions Judge. Member of the Special Tribunal that tried U Saw. After independence, Judge of the High Court.

Justice Thaung Sein. Born in 1906 in Syriam. A member of the ICS, serving concurrently as Secretary in the Ministry of Judicial Affairs and Inspector

General of Prisons in 1947. Judge of the High Court from independence in 1948 until his retirement in 1962. Emigrated to Australia in 1975. Died in 1989 in Melbourne.

Maj.-Gen. Tun Hla Oung. Born in 1902 in Rangoon. Member of the Imperial Police and Deputy Inspector General of the Criminal Investigation Department. Credited with the rapid capture of U Saw and his men. Jointly responsible for U Saw's security together with Justice Thaung Sein. Inspector General of Police after Burma's independence and promoted to Deputy Supreme Commander with the rank of Major-General in August 1948. Died in 1960 in Rangoon.

Curtis-Bennett, Frederick Henry (Derek). Born in 1904. A King's Counsel from Britain employed by U Saw to assist in his defence. Found dead in his London flat in July 1956.

Vertannes, Benjamin Raphael. A former army captain and pleader in the Rangoon High Court who became junior defence counsel for U Saw. Originally from Burma, he retired and moved to Britain after independence.

Busk, Michael E. Ex-Chindit (World War Two veteran). Assistant Commissioner of Police in Rangoon in the late 1940s. Had earlier raised a battalion of Kachin tribesmen in Myitkyina for the Armed Police. Arrested Capt. David Vivian (see below).

Tooke, Colin. Born in 1913. With the Burma Police from 1933. District Superintendent of Police; Hanthawaddy, 1945–6. Believed to have been secretly investigating U Saw's case, when his files were stolen. Died suddenly in 1948.

The Politicians

Aung Gyi. Born in 1919 in Paungde. Joined the anti-Japanese struggle in 1945 as one of Ne Win's officers. Later served under Ne Win in the 4th Burma Rifles. Organiser of the Socialist Party. Member of the Revolutionary Council when Ne Win seized power in 1962. Ousted in 1963. Re-entered politics during the 1988 pro-democracy uprising.

Dr. Ba Maw. Born in 1897 in a Christian family; said to be partly Armenian. Educated at Cambridge and Bordeaux (Ph.D). Schoolmaster and barrister. Formed the *Sinyetha Wunthanu* Party; Prime Minister 1936–9. Head of the Japanese-sponsored government during World War Two. Interned in 1947. Died in May 1977.

Thakin Ba Sein. Born in 1910. Educated at Rangoon University. Student leader and one of the founders of the *Dohbama Asiayone* in the 1930s. Sympathetic to the Axis powers during World War Two; Burmese ambassador to Manchukuo. Accompanied Aung San to London in 1947. Right-wing politician.

U Ba Swe. Born in 1915 in Tavoy. Educated at Rangoon University. Student leader in the 1930s. President of the Socialist Party in 1945, but resigned in favour of Thakin Mya. Socialist leader again after Thakin Mya's assassination. Prime Minister for a brief period in 1956–7. Arrested after Ne Win's takeover in 1962. Released in 1966 and died in December 1987.

Bo Khin Maung Gale. Born in 1912 in Toungoo. Educated at Rangoon University. Schoolmaster and officer in the Burma Independence Army. Founder-member of the Socialist Party. Held several portfolios in U Nu's governments in the 1950s. Arrested after Ne Win's takeover in 1962. Released in 1966 and died in September 1985.

U Kyaw Nyein. Born in 1915 in Pyinmana. Educated at Rangoon University and student leader in the 1930s. Succeeded Thakin Than Tun as General Secretary of the Anti-Fascist People's Freedom League in 1946. Minister for Home and Judicial Affairs. Leader of the Socialist Party. Arrested after Ne Win's takeover in 1962. Released in 1966 and died in Rangoon in June 1986.

U Nu (*aka*) **Thakin Nu**. Born in 1907 in Wakema. Student leader and one of the founders of the *Dohbama Asiayone* in the 1930s. Prime Minister, July 1947 and remained head of most governments during Burma's democratic period. Overthrown by Ne Win in 1962 and arrested. Released in 1966 and went into exile to organise resistance against Ne Win's military government. Returned during an amnesty in 1980. Took part in the 1988 uprising for democracy and on 9 September proclaimed an interim government with himself as Prime Minister; under house arrest from December 1989 to April 1992. Died in Rangoon in February 1995.

Thakin Shu Maung, alias Bo Ne Win. Born in 1911 in Paungdale near Prome. Educated at Judson College in Rangoon but left without a degree in 1931. Post office clerk and member of the *Dohbama Asiayone*. One of the Thirty Comrades and commander of the Burma National Army, 1943–5. Commander in Chief of the army 1949–72. Seized power in a *coup d'état* in 1962. Chairman of "the Revolutionary Council" 1962–74; President 1974–81 and Chairman of the Burma Socialist Programme Party 1962–88. Believed to be still the actual ruler of Burma.

Thakin Than Tun. Born in 1915 in Pyinmana. Village schoolmaster; married to Daw Khin Khin Gyi, the sister of Aung San's wife, Daw Khin Kyi. General Secretary of the Anti-Fascist People's Freedom League until 1946; leader of the Communist Party of Burma, which in March 1948 operated as an underground party in active rebellion against the central government. Assassinated in 1968 at his headquarters in the jungles of the Pegu Yoma.

U Tin Tut. Born in 1895. Educated at Dulwich College and Cambridge University. Member of the Indian Civil Service and Vice-Chancellor of Rangoon University. Minister in several cabinets until he resigned in 1948 to edit the *New Times of Burma*. Assassinated in December 1948. Justice Kyaw Myint's brother.

Thakin Tun Oke. Born in 1907. Educated in Rangoon and Colombo. Leader of one faction of the *Dohbama Asiayone* (together with Thakin Ba Sein; Ne Win also belonged to this faction). Author of *Kyun-noke-to-ei-sunsaghan* ("Our Exploits") which was written along the lines of Hitler's *Mein Kampf*. Went to Japan in 1940; right-wing opposition politician in the 1940s and 1950s. Died in January 1970.

The Colonial Authorities

Dorman-Smith, Sir Reginald Hugh. Born in 1899. Conservative MP, 1935-41; minister in several British cabinets. Governor of Burma, 1941–6. Knew U Saw well.

Laithwaite, Sir John Gilbert. Born in 1894. Joined the India Office in 1919; private secretary to the Viceroy 1936–43. Deputy Under-Secretary of State for Burma 1945–8.

Listowel, the 5th Earl of (William Francis Hare). Born in 1906. Secretary of State for India and Burma from April 1947; for Burma only, August 1947–January 1948. Close to Bo Ne Win of the 4th Burma Rifles.

Mountbatten, Viscount Mountbatten of Burma (Rear-Admiral Lord Louis Francis Albert Victor Nicholas). Born in 1900. Supreme Allied Commander, Southeast Asia, 1943–6; Viceroy of India, March–August 1947 and then Governor-General of India. Favoured Aung San as leader of independent Burma.

Rance, Major General Sir Hubert. Born in 1898. With the UK Western Command 1943–5; Director of Civil Affairs, Burma, 1945–6. The last Governor of Burma, August 1946–January 1948. Neutral between the different political factions in Burma.

Who Were They?

Bingley, John Stewart. Born in 1899. British Council representative in Rangoon 1946–7. U Saw, from his cell in Insein Jail, wrote several letters to him, asking for money. Left Burma in a hurry on 4 September 1947. Whereabouts unknown.

Daine, Major Peter Ernest Lancelot. Born in 1923. Indian Signal Corps; first commissioned in 1944. With the Intelligence Branch, Burma Command HQ in 1947. Commander, Base Ammunition Depot north of Mingaladon. He was not arrested.

Moore, Major J.A. Born in 1908. Indian Army Ordnance Corps. Officer Commanding at the Base Ammunition Depot, Botataung. He was arrested but not sentenced.

Vivian, Captain David. First commissioned in 1932. Seconded from the Indian Army to act as Arms Adviser to the Burma Police. Arrested on 20 July and charged with selling arms to U Saw. Sentenced to five years' imprisonment and two fines of 5,000 Rupees each. Set free when Karen insurgents occupied Insein in February 1949. Joined the Karen rebels. The Burmese authorities still assume that he was killed along with Karen rebel chief Saw Ba U Gyi at Kawkareik near the Thai border in August 1950. But he was not in Saw Ba U Gyi's camp that day; he stayed with the Karen insurgents for several years until he returned to Britain via Thailand in the mid-1950s. Died in Swansea, Wales, in the late 1980s.

Young, Major C. Henry. Commander of Indian Army Electrical and Mechanical Engineers (IAEME) Workshop Company. Arrested on 24 August 1947 for supplying arms to U Saw. Sentenced to two years' imprisonment, but acquitted on appeal. Left Burma immediately.

Notes on Names in Burma

There are no family names in Burma but it is considered impolite not to use an honorific when addressing a person. *U, Ko* and *Maung* mean "mister" of different grades according to rank and age (in that descending order) as well as kinship. Thus, Nu would be called *Maung* Nu by his mother, *Ko* Nu by his friends, and *U* Nu when addressed formally or by subordinates. *Daw* and *Ma* perform the same functions in regard to women. *Daw* Aung San Suu Kyi is the formal designation while *Ma* Aung San Suu Kyi would be used when she was younger or by her friends. *Bo* and *Bohmu* are military titles for officers which are often carried into civilian life, like *Bogyoke*, which means "Supremo" or "Chief" and is more respectful than "General", a military designation only. *Bogyokegyi* means "Great Supremo" and is a title reserved for Aung San. *Thakin* is a title used by the young nationalists in the 1930s (*Thakin* Nu, for instance); it means "master" and was originally reserved for the British. Members of Shan princely families are titled *Sao*. Pwo Karens are titled *Mahn* and Sgaw Karens *Saw* (not to be confused with the Burman name Saw, as in U Saw or Gen. Saw Maung).

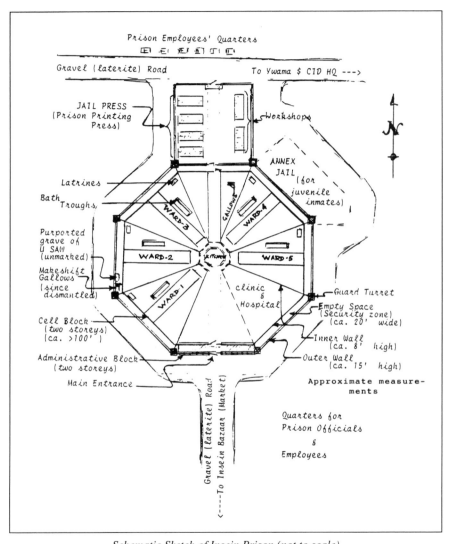

Schematic Sketch of Insein Prison (not to scale)
Here U Saw was incarcerated, tried and hanged in 1947–48, and the purported gravesite.

1

The General Has Been Shot

It was the Burmese month of Wagaung, when good Buddhists observe Lent and the rice fields are flooded by the rains, promising bountiful harvests. As dawn broke on the morning of the 19th, a storm was brewing under cloudy monsoon skies. A group of young men had gathered outside the No. 4 Ady Road residence of U Saw, a senior Burmese politician. His trim compound was located on a peninsula in the tranquil Inya Lake in an exclusive suburb on the northern outskirts of Burma's capital Rangoon. U Saw himself was awake to give final instructions to his followers: they were just about to set out on a mission that was to change Burma forever. One of U Saw's young men, his wife's nephew, Khin Maung Yin, climbed into the cabin of a green Fordson truck and took the wheel. Three other youthful disciples of the veteran politician also jumped into the truck. They left the compound at 8.30 a.m.

No one paid much attention to them as they drove towards central Rangoon; World War Two had just ended and military-looking vehicles were no strange sight in the Burmese capital. Half an hour later, the Fordson truck stopped near the Secretariat, a two-storey, Victorian red-brick building in central Rangoon. Maung Ni, a member of the team, remained with the vehicle while it was parked at the corner of Dalhousie and 41st Streets. Khin Maung Yin and his two companions, Ba Nyunt and Hmon Gyi, walked into the actual Secretariat area complex to reconnoitre. They wanted to make sure that the Executive Council was really going to be in session later that morning. It was. Khin Maung Yin, using a telephone in the building, rang his master to deliver a curt message: "Piston rings received."

On receiving the coded confirmation, a jeep took off immediately from U Saw's residence on Ady Road. It was now 10 a.m. Beside the driver, Thu Kha, sat Maung

Soe, a tall man in his thirties. Crouched under the canvas-covered rear of the vehicle were three young gunmen: Maung Sein, Thet Hnin and Yan Gyi Aung. Maung Soe, Maung Sein, and Thet Hnin were armed with a Tommy gun each, while young Yan Gyi Aung, a teenager, carried a semi-automatic Sten. Another Tommy gun lay on the floor in the jeep; it was meant for Ba Nyunt, who was waiting at the Secretariat. The men were dressed in jungle-green fatigues and floppy bush hats. On the shoulders of their uniforms were the insignia of the XIIth Army, Burma's original war-time garrison army. Two pieces of red and white bunting fluttered from the left corner of the windscreen as the jeep sped towards the city centre.

Almost simultaneously, Bogyoke Aung San—the 32-year-old leader of Burma's nationalist movement and Deputy Chairman of the Executive Council, or, in effect, Prime Minister of the pre-independence cabinet—started out in a chauffeur-driven car from his home in Tower Lane, a green, lush suburb close to Rangoon's Royal Lakes. He had discarded his military uniform, which he had worn when he was *Bogyoke*, or General, for civilian clothes: a white collarless shirt, a crisp silk jacket, and a gold-coloured silk *longyi*. Living closer to the Secretariat than U Saw at Ady Road, he reached the office in his chauffeur-driven car well before the armed men arrived there. The other Councillors too made their way to the Secretariat to assemble for what they expected to be a routine meeting of the pre-independence Cabinet. The country's independence had been negotiated with Britain, the colonial power, and freedom was less than six months away.

Meanwhile, Ba Nyunt, although unarmed, was searching the premises to see if he could find one of the intended victims: Aung San's close associate, Thakin Nu, the Speaker of the Constituent Assembly, as the pre-independence parliament was called. Ba Nyunt passed through the central, high-arched throughway of the main building. He glanced through the window of Thakin Nu's office, the first cubicle in the West Wing of the new Constituent Assembly Hall, which was located in the court of the quadrangle of the Secretariat. Ba Nyunt saw the top part of the face of a person sitting there. He looked closely. It was not Thakin Nu. Ba Nyunt left the building. Walking briskly back towards the truck, he slipped into a tea shop and sat down. Khin Maung Yin, who was loitering in the vicinity, spotted Ba Nyunt sipping his cup of tea and came over to tell him about the coded message to the Boss. Everything was going according to plan.

Khin Maung Yin continued on to the Fordson truck, which was parked at a nearby vantage point. Suddenly, he spotted the jeep carrying their armed comrades. "They have arrived," he signalled to Ba Nyunt, who lowered his teacup and looked around anxiously. As the jeep approached the Secretariat's central porchway, the only obstacle seemed to be a truck moving in front of it. The jeep slowed down and waited for the truck to drive away. The route was then clear. No one made any attempt to search the jeep or its occupants.

The Councillors took their seats in Aung San's chamber, which was located upstairs in the West Wing of the building. A series of tables, placed together in the form of an inverted U, were reserved for the Council in the southern end of the room. Aung San sat down in the centre of the top end of the table arrangement and greeted his fellow ministers. Sitting to the left of him was my uncle U Shwe Baw, the Secretary of the Council, and on his right, U Ohn Maung, a ministerial deputy secretary.

At the adjacent table on the right were the familiar faces of Thakin Mya, the Socialist leader who served as Councillor of Finance; U Abdul Razak, a Muslim politician and Councillor of Education and National Planning; U Ba Win, Aung San's elder brother and Councillor of Commerce and Supplies; U Ba Choe, a well-known journalist and editor of the *Deedok* magazine, who now served as Councillor of Information; and Mahn Ba Khaing, Councillor of Industry and Labour and a leader of the Karen ethnic minority.

Seated at the table to the left of Aung San were the Councillor of Public Works, U Ba Gyan; Social Services Councillor U Aung Zan Wai; U Mya, the Councillor for Agriculture; and Sao Sam Htun, the *sawbwa*, or prince, of the Shan state of Möng Pawn, who served as Councillor for the Frontier Areas. He had played an important role in the efforts to amalgamate the minority-inhabited frontier areas with Burma proper.

All were seated facing inwards and looking towards Aung San when the day's session began at 10.30 a.m. But the meeting was almost immediately interrupted by U Ohn Maung, a deputy secretary in the Department of Transport and Communications, who stepped in. There was an urgent matter he had to clarify on behalf of his minister, Saw San Po Thin, who was away on duty upcountry that morning. U Ohn Maung requested the assembly to let him clear up his assignment first as he was not actually on duty that day and had something important to do later.

All the doors of the room, except the one in the north directly opposite the office of the Councillor for Public Works, were closed and bolted from the inside. And there, the peon Thaung Sein stood guard. He was unarmed; the only mark of the young man's authority was perhaps the green trousers he wore.

Further down the corridor, U Tin Ohn, the assistant secretary of the Council, was standing talking to a friend—when suddenly he heard the clatter of guns as four armed men came hurrying up the stairway. As they walked briskly towards Aung San's office, they were also spotted by U Htin Baw, a clerk working in the Secretariat. In the lead was Maung Soe, easily recognisable by his taller height and longish face. Yan Gyi Aung, a teenager, was conspicuous by his youthfulness. Hmon Gyi, who had remained in and around the Secretariat since early morning, was there waiting for them. He nodded to the gunmen to signal that the meeting was now in progress.

When Maung Soe approached the only open door, the young peon Thaung Sein was taken by surprise. He rushed forward and tried to block the entrance. Maung Soe and Thet Hnin pointed their Tommy guns at him. He was pushed aside and lost his balance, but bravely followed the gunmen as they entered the room. They pointed their weapons at the assembled ministers, shouting: "Don't run away! Don't get up!" As Aung San rose to his feet, Maung Soe gave the order: "Fire!" The *Bogyokegyi* fell to the floor, blood streaming from the wounds of thirteen bullets.

Maung Soe, Maung Sein, and Thet Hnin continued to spray the Councillors with bullets from their Tommy guns. Yan Gyi Aung knelt down and shot with his Sten gun at those who had fallen or were trying to duck for cover under the tables. After 30 seconds of incessant shooting, Maung Soe ordered his men to beat a retreat.

It was 10.37 a.m. Bo Tun Hla, Aung San's personal assistant, and Lieut. Than Win, Aide-de-Camp to the GOC, Burma Command, were the first to arrive on the scene. Other people in the Secretariat were soon jostling in the open doorway. The pungent smell of cordite and fumes of heavy smoke filled the room, but the victims were clearly seen. The tables and chairs were overturned and soiled with blood. Aung San, our *Bogyokegyi* and national hero, lay dead on the floor, killed at the age of 32. Thakin Mya's lungs had been punctured by a hail of bullets, and he too lay dead, huddled in a pool of blood under one of the tables. Abdul Razak had taken six bullets, U Ba Win eight, and Mahn Ba Khaing as many as fifteen. They were all lifeless, their bodies slumped forward in their chairs.

Aung San had obviously been the main target of the assassins. After shooting him, the gunmen appeared to have swung to the right, finishing off each of the Councillors, who must have frozen in their chairs. The only one cut down by the assassins' bullets on the table to the left was Sao Sam Htun, closest to the assailants. He had remained seated. Among the others at his table, U Shwe Baw and U Mya had miraculously survived by rushing to a side door of the chamber.

Shwe Baw had managed to open it—only to faint and fall ▓
Mya on top of him. U Aung Zan Wai and U Ba Gyan, who ▓
floor, escaped almost unscathed; the latter was hit in the right ri▓
seemed to be a ricocheting bullet.

Razak was breathing feebly, but these were his last gasps. U Ba Ch▓
been struck by five bullets, including one in the brain, was still alive▓
rushed to hospital together with Sao Sam Htun, hit twice in the head and▓
sitting on the floor, bleeding from the mouth and pitifully gesticulating for w▓
The bullet-ridden body of U Ohn Maung, the secretary who had come to deliver▓
report, was found on the floor: he had died on the spot.

Maung Than, a newspaper reporter, had rushed out of the press room when he
heard the noise. The retreating gunmen spotted him and screamed at him to stop.
Maung Than promptly threw himself on the floor and then looked up to see Ko
Htwe, U Razak's bodyguard, run out from his room to prevent the gunmen from
escaping. Yan Gyi Aung was now in the lead. Without warning, he blasted away
with his Sten gun. The young bodyguard took four bullets and fell to the floor.
Like Yan Gyi Aung, Ko Htwe was a teenager.

Shouting "Victory! Victory!" the gunmen dashed out of the building. Thu Kha
had already driven the jeep up to a spot near the stairway of the Secretariat and
kept the engine running. The assassins leapt into the vehicle. Thu Kha stepped on
the accelerator—but with such ferocity that the engine shuddered to a halt. Maung
Sein pushed him aside and, with some effort, managed to start the engine again.
Thu Kha put the jeep in gear and accelerated away.

Maung Ni was at his post at the exit gate on Sparks Street. His duty was to
intervene, using his revolver, should the escape of the gang prove difficult. But
again, no problems arose, except that Maung Ni, contrary to orders, then tried
unsuccessfully to board the jeep, which was moving at 50 k.p.h. U Sein Maung, a
diligent reporter from the Thamadi Press, observed the spectacle from nearby. He
quickly jotted down the vehicle's number on a bank pay-in slip, which he happened to have in his pocket.

The jeep turned at high speed into Dalhousie Street and proceeded east. Going
north along the Stockade Road, Maung Sein became impatient with Thu Kha's
driving, which wasn't fast enough. He took over and drove furiously along the
roads leading up to the northern suburbs, and into the narrow, winding Ady Road.
Captain H. Khan, one of U Saw's neighbours, was about to drive out of his

at on the floor, with U
had lain flat on the
g finger by what
e, who had
and was
found
ter.

/oid a head-on collision with the speeding
icle that had almost hit him, saw it turn
in Inya Lake further down the road. He
ss the lake to U Saw's garden. He saw
whom he recognised as U Saw himself. It

ivy-blue shorts, seemed elated. He was
em for a job well done. Waving their
d once again: *"Aung Byi! Aung Byi"*!—
, with feasting and drinking. The party
ng Yin and Maung Ni returned in their
among those shot?" U Saw demanded. Ba Nyunt
had to admit that he was not, and related the circumstances. U Saw nodded and accepted the explanation. He did not seem overly concerned about Thakin Nu. The main task, to eliminate Aung San, had been accomplished. With the main leader of the Burmese nationalists out of the way, U Saw expected a call at any minute from the British Governor, Sir Hubert Rance, requesting him to form a new cabinet. U Saw was Aung San's main political rival and contender for power. He was well connected in high places and had followers among civil servants as well as in the army. Other politicians were considered too young and inexperienced. At 47, U Saw was a veteran of the game. He was the owner and editor of the *Sun* newspaper, the leader of the *Myochit* ("Patriots") Party, and had served as Prime Minister from 1940 to 1942, before the Japanese occupation.

But it was not U Saw who was summoned to form a new cabinet that day. At 11 a.m., U Tin of the daily *Myanma Alin* ("The New Light of Burma") had phoned Thakin Nu, one of the intended victims, who luckily had not been present at the time of the assassination. When Thakin Nu learned from the newspaper man about the killings, he rushed to the Secretariat, only to find that the bodies had already been removed to Rangoon General Hospital. Thakin Nu went there, looked upon the corpse of Aung San—whom he had met the previous evening—and was choked with tears. It was about 1 p.m. when Thakin Nu arrived back at his residence on Lewis Road. He was then told that the leaders of the Anti-Fascist People's Freedom League (AFPFL), the main political party in Burma at the time, were waiting for him at the adjoining headquarters of the People's Volunteer Organisation (PVO), an association for war-time veterans, which, in effect, had became a militia force loyal to Aung San.

As Thakin Nu appeared at the PVO office, Thakin Tin greeted him: "Trouble will befall the whole nation if U Saw is appointed in General Aung San's place. You must see the Governor so that you can fill the General's position." Only five members of the 11-man Governor's Executive Council remained: the three survivors from that morning's shooting—U Ba Gyan, U Aung Zan Wai, and U Mya— plus Transport and Communications Councillor, Saw San Po Thin, and Kyaw Nyein, the Councillor for Home and Judicial Affairs.

Thakin Nu did not hesitate. The AFPFL's executive committee passed a resolution recommending him for the post of Deputy Chairman of the Executive Council to replace Aung San. Thakin Nu agreed on condition that he would be allowed to resign six months after independence.

Shortly afterwards, when Thakin Nu had returned home, the Governor called him. Thakin Nu was officially invited to become Prime Minister and form a government. Sir Hubert Rance also recommended that a compassionate grant of 100,000 Rupees be made to the widow of each martyr. Aung San left behind his wife, Daw Khin Kyi, and three small children: two sons Aung San Oo and Aung San Lin[1] and a two-year-old daughter Aung San Suu Kyi.

The midday heat, the strain of the day—and the drinks they had consumed— made the men in U Saw's compound doze off into an afternoon siesta, blissfully unaware of what was happening elsewhere in the city. They were awakened just before 3 p.m. by the roar of car engines on the road outside. Police and paramilitary forces had surrounded U Saw's residence. Maung Soe at once grabbed for his gun, but those near him prevented him from using it. Hmon Gyi, however, raised his Tommy gun only to be shot in the hand by the police. Other followers were meanwhile hastily throwing the guns that had been used that morning into Inya Lake behind the house, where U Saw had built a family shrine on stilts in the water.

The fall from the giddy heights of triumph and victory to being caught more or less red-handed for murder in less than a day would have upset the mental equilibrium of most people. But U Saw was a rare exception. His composure during the entire police raid was totally calm. He seemed confident that everything would work out to his advantage in the end. Sipping whisky from a glass in his hand, he nonchalantly asked to see the police superintendent's search warrant. Only after the evidently nervous officer had phoned his superiors and received verbal orders to proceed, did U Saw permit him to search the house. Throughout the search, U Saw continued to sip whisky. He maintained an air of authority with the policemen, and cajoled his men to allay their fears, acting like a father to his children in the Burmese way.

U Saw remained jovial and seemed unmoved even when the police discovered some guns and ammunition still in his house: a 9-mm sub-machine gun, a Sten gun and some ammunition. Both weapons were owned by U Saw under licence, but they were nevertheless confiscated as evidence. "What's next?" U Saw demanded, smiling. The stern-faced officer made another phone call and came up to U Saw: "You are under arrest. And you will be taken into safe custody immediately." U Saw turned to his followers, still unshaken by events: "Pack your bedding and don't forget to bring enough blankets. The authorities at the place we're going to may not be able to supply us with as many as we need." He added casually: "We may all have to be 'away' for three or four days. Nothing to worry about."

Daw Than Khin, U Saw's wife, was not at home that day; she was staying with her first husband's uncle in Insein, just north of Rangoon. But there were two women in U Saw's house on 19 July: Khin Maung Yin's and Maung Ni's wives. They were left alone, as were two servants, a young boy and a girl.

My father, Tun Hla Oung, who in his capacity as Deputy Inspector General of the Criminal Investigation Department was the second highest-ranking police officer in Burma at the time, arrived on the scene as the men were being led into police vehicles. The swift police action which he ordered had been prompted by a tip-off from Captain Khan. After he had almost been hit by the gunmen's jeep, Khan had gone straight to Tun Hla Oung's residence in Windermere Park. Not finding him there, Khan had rung the CID chief's office at 1 p.m.

Tun Hla Oung pensively inspected the seized weapons. Some rather odd paraphernalia were also found in the house: freshly printed stationery, rubber seals, and stamps with U Saw's name—accompanied by the title "Prime Minister". The CID chief then turned his attention to the cars in the compound. There were two jeeps and he tried to start the engines. Only one had a hood, and it bore a number plate with conspicuously fresh paint. It started easily, but not the other. A Fordson truck was parked in the garage.

U Saw's attempt at *thoke-thin-ye*, as the Burmese saying goes—to remove rivals by complete elimination in order to wrest the crown and ascend the throne— thus came to an abrupt end. Instead of receiving an emissary from the Governor to escort him to his Residence, U Saw and his cohorts were whisked away to prison in a Black Maria. It was dusk when the doors of Insein Jail closed on the conspirators later that day.

16

News of the carnage in the Secretariat had sped through the city and the nation was plunged into grief. Apart from the six officials who had died on the spot in the Secretariat, there were three further fatalities. U Ba Choe succumbed to his wounds that afternoon and Sao Sam Htun expired the following day, while Ko Htwe, the young bodyguard, died a few days later. Nine men in all had lost their lives to satisfy the greed and lust for power of a single politician. Burma's most competent leaders, who had been preparing to take over from the British, were dead before the country had even become independent.

Maj.-Gen. Tun Hla Oung, Inspector-General of Police and Deputy-Supreme Commander, August 1948

Maj.-Gen. Aung San, Commander of the Burmese Defence Army. (Invested with the 'Order of the Rising Sun' by Emperor Hirohito in Japan, 1943).

Colonel Ne Win, Chief of Staff of the Burma Defence Army, 1942–43.

Above: Maj.-Gen. and Mrs. Tun Hla Oung.

Right: Maha Thiri Thudamma Justice and Mrs. Thaung Sein.

The Governor's Executive Council appointed on 27 September 1946. Front row L to R: Thakin Ba Sein, Bogyoke Aung San, Maj.-Gen. Sir Hubert E Rance, U Ba Pe, U Tin Tut. Back row L to R: Thakin Mya, U Aung Zan Wai and Thakin Thein Pe.

The Governor's Executive Council, after the assassination. Seated L to R: Kyaw Nyein, Sir Ba U, Lady Rance, Thakin Nu, Sir Hubert Rance, The Earl of Listowel (Secretary of State for Burma), Bo Let Ya, Sir Gilbert Laithwaite, U Tin Tut, Standing front L to R: Mr. R.E. McGuire, Mahn Win Maung, Bo Po Kun, four ADCs, Thakin Tin, Henzada U Mya, Vum Ko Hau, Miss Wakefield, Back L to R: Mr. J.L. Leyden, Pyawbwe U Mya, Sir Ralph Stoneham, U Ba Gyan, C.F.B. Pearce and Mr. Harris.

"Galon" U Saw, former Prime Minister and alleged ringleader, in the witness box at the trial at the court of the Special Tribunal in Insein Jail.

In the dock at the trial: Alleged assassins Maung Soe, Thet Hnin, Sein Gyi, and Yan Gyi Aung; and alleged accomplices Thu Kha, Khin Maung Yin, Maung Ni, and Hmon Gyi.

Midshipman Kin Oung, Burma R.N.V.R. 1945–46.

Kin Oung at an "8.8.88 Massacre" Rally with Saw Lwin Oo, in front of the SLORC Embassy in Canberra, Australia, 1991.

'Xmas at Oxford'. In Aung San Suu Kyi's home with family and friends (Circa 1983).

2

The Martyrs

The men who were gunned down mercilessly in the Secretariat on 19 July 1947 were among the finest of modern Burma's statesmen. They had been destined to lead Burma into its final year of British rule, though, alas, not to complete independence. The struggle they led had actually begun as soon as the British marched into Mandalay in 1885, ending the last of the Burmese Kingdoms and completing the conquest that had begun with the First Anglo-Burmese War of 1824–6. The King was led away in captivity and sent into exile in India, but the Royal Army, some of the surviving princes, court officials, village headmen and even Buddhist monks took up the sword in many regions of the old Burmese Kingdom, which had now become a province of British India. John F. Cady wrote in his *A History of Modern Burma*:

> Throughout 1886 and 1887, every district of Upper Burma was in a ferment of revolt. Military posts and convoys were attacked, and virtually every male villager was ready to fight. The population accepted the hardships of war and enveloped all rebel movements in a conspiracy of silence.

In the view of the Burmese, these men were brave patriots, but the British branded the fighters "dacoits", or bandits, and meted out summary justice to them. A year after the British conquest, Sir Charles Crosthwaite, an extremely harsh administrator, was appointed Chief Commissioner of Burma. He mounted a merciless campaign to suppress the rebellions. Mass executions of so-called dacoits took place and villages showing any sympathy for the freedom fighters were promptly put to the torch. Not even women and children were spared; the total number of people killed in battle or executed on being captured, by hangings or decapitation, numbered in the thousands. Aung San's maternal grand-uncle, Bo Min Yaung, led one of these local resistance armies; he was among those captured and decapitated by the British.

It took the British five years and the deployment of 60,000 regular troops and military police to stamp out the insurrections in the north. They could hardly have imagined that such action would be necessary to subdue the people when they had first marched into Mandalay with just 500 men.

The spirit of nationalism then went into the doldrums for almost two decades, as all leading resistance fighters had been eliminated. But even after Burma had been "pacified", to use the colonial jargon, there were local uprisings in the Chindwin and Monywa districts, and skirmishes with small bands of guerrillas never ceased.

But by 1904, new nationalist leaders had begun to emerge from the youthful ranks of Rangoon College, working hand-in-hand with others who had set up the first politicised Buddhist societies as early as 1897. The Young Men's Buddhist Association (YMBA) was founded in 1906 by 26 college students, among them U Ba Pe, U Hla Pe, U Ba Dun, and U Maung Maung Gyi, an MA holder. In 1908, at a YMBA meeting at Daw Mya May's Queen Victoria Memorial Girls' High School in Rangoon, young English-educated barristers like U Maung Kin (later knighted) and U May Oung—my maternal and paternal grandfathers—and U Thein Maung, and others joined the fledgling nationalist movement. Soon thereafter senior government servants and more barristers became members. Within a decade, the YMBA had established itself as a national body and the original plan for a more firmly organised movement crystallised into the General Council of Buddhist Associations (GCBA) in 1917.

The first open challenge to the colonial authorities came from the students in Rangoon in December 1920. A bill had been introduced which would provide Burma with its first resident university, replacing two colleges that had previously been subordinate to the University of Calcutta. The students and other nationalists had reservations about some details of the bill, including matriculation requirements and tuition costs—but the British Lieutenant-Governor, Sir Reginald Craddock, turned a deaf ear to the demands. The bill was passed in its original version as the Rangoon University Act on 1 December. Four days later, 500 of the 600 students in Rangoon launched a strike, which was followed by strikes by high school pupils in the capital as well as in Mandalay and other towns. Despite threats by the Lieutenant-Governor, the public at large helped the strikers enthusiastically. Not all their demands were met, but the strike ignited a strong flame of nationalism which could not be extinguished.

The first national leader to emerge during these first tumultuous years of the reborn Burmese nationalist movement was Sayadaw U Ottama, an

Arakanese monk who had spent some time in India and Tokyo. He returned to Burma in 1919 and began travelling extensively, preaching patriotism and organising *Wunthanu Athins* ("Nationalist Societies") across the country. The Imperial Government responded fiercely, bringing in the military police to break up these groups.

U Ottama himself was arrested in 1921 because of his militant speeches: he was tried for sedition and sentenced to 18 months' imprisonment. The impact of this sentence could be felt all over Burma. It was the first time a nationalist had been charged with sedition and, adding insult to injury, he was a Buddhist monk of the eminence of a *sayadaw*, or great teacher: it was a challenge to the dignity of the entire nation. U Ottama was to spend several more spells in prison before his death on 9 September 1939.

Other prominent Buddhist monks also took part in the movement. Sayadaw U Wisara was one of them. Born in 1888 in Monywa, he had entered monkhood at the age of 20 and later organised the *Sangha Sammeggi Aphwe* ("the United Monks' Organisation"). Helped by U Ottama, U Wisara also went to study in India and, on his return to Burma, he gave political speeches in the villages in the countryside. He too was arrested, released and re-arrested. While awaiting trial, he went on a hunger strike for 40 days. The physically—but not mentally— weakened *sayadaw* was sentenced to a year and nine months rigorous imprisonment.

He was forcefully disrobed and told to wear ordinary convict apparel, which he refused to do. He was then placed naked in solitary confinement, and thereafter followed a cruel cycle of hunger strikes, spells in solitary confinement, and force-feeding. The authorities went as far as to confine him to Rangoon's notorious Tadagale lunatic asylum. After spending seven months there, he was sent to Rangoon's Central Jail, and his stubborn resistance continued. Following another hunger strike, he was sentenced to six years' hard labour. U Wisara went on a fast again. An appeal for mercy was turned down by the Burman Home Member, Joseph Augustus Maung Gyi.

Eventually, on 19 September 1929, on the 166th day of his last fast, U Wisara passed away. Today, his bronze statue stands on a prominent roundabout near the Shwe Dagon Pagoda in Rangoon, and the road leading up to it, which was previously called Tiger Alley, has now been renamed U Wisara Road. He and U Ottama were the best known of the *sayadaws* opposing the colonial regime and they paved the way for the participation by the Buddhist clergy in the nationalist movement, a crucial factor in its eventual success.

In the year that Sayadaw U Wisara died, an ex-monk called U Yar Kyaw, a member of the GCBA, was setting up branches of a new secret society in the countryside called *Galon Athins*. They were similar to U Ottama's *Wunthanu Athins* but much more masonic in their organisation and way of operating. The *galon* was a powerful bird in Hindu mythology—the garuda in Sanskrit—and these groups attracted many village youths and others from the impoverished countryside, which the splendours of the colonial economy never reached. The people were poor and they were desperate.

In the meantime, Joseph Augustus Maung Gyi had been awarded a knighthood and become the first Burman acting Governor (deputising for Sir Charles Innes, who was on home leave in Britain due to illness). Sir Joseph went to the worst affected area, the district of Tharrawaddy north of Rangoon, and held a durbar in the town, as he had done in many other places before. At the public audience on 21 December 1930, peasant representatives pleaded to the acting Governor to cancel or at least postpone tax collection in the rural areas for a year. Sir Joseph, however, imperiously rejected the request. The following day, a rebellion broke out among the peasants of Tharrawaddy.

Their leader was U Yar Kyaw, who now was known as Saya San. He had proclaimed himself King, assuming the title of *thupannaka galuna raja* ("the Illustrious Galon King"), and raised an army of disgruntled peasants. With almost bare hands they decided to face the modern guns of the British colonial army: the arsenal of the rebels consisted of no more than thirty firearms, supplemented by hand-made shotguns manufactured from pipe-lengths and bicycle tubing. Apart from this, they had only cross-bows and spears. According to US Professor Lucien W. Pye:

> The Saya San rebellion which broke out in 1930 conformed to the traditional Burmese political and religious pattern of revolts which sought to establish a new monarchy. Guided by soothsayers and supported by magicians, tattooers and the sellers of protective medicines, amulets and charms, the army raised by Saya San placed him upon a throne under the White Umbrella, which symbolised royalty in old Burma, and convinced themselves that they were invulnerable to mere modern guns and weapons. The movement thrived on ignorance, superstition and readiness to accept a mystical and magical view of the universe, to live on unreasonable and emotional expectations of political success.

The majority of the fighters in Saya San's *galon* army had risen to recover their land from the hands of money-lenders who had taken over vast tracts of the

Burmese countryside during the repression of the early 1930s. They may have been naive, but their grievances were real, and, as Burmese historian Dr. Htin Aung, pointed out: "The only way for the people of Tharrawaddy to end their misery was to rise in rebellion against the British . . . [and] was death not preferable to this misery of poverty under an alien rule?"

Saya San first raised his standard at Alan-taung—which literally means "the-hill-where-the-flag-flew"—in the Pegu Yoma mountain range north of Rangoon, east of Tharrawaddy. A whole battalion of British troops were thrown in against the *galons*. Saya San's headquarters fell and casualties were extremely heavy. But the insurrection spread to 12 out of 40 districts, from its epicentre in Tharrawaddy down to the Irrawaddy delta and north to Upper Burma and even to some parts of the Shan states. The government's forces resorted to brutal suppression: entire villages were razed to the ground, suspected rebels were decapitated and their severed heads displayed as a warning to others. In one particularly gruesome incident, 15 severed heads were displayed in front of the Deputy Commissioner's office in Prome. Photographs of the gory exhibition appeared in the *Sun* newspaper, owned and edited by U Saw, and copies were sent to the British parliament.

When the uprising was finally crushed, more than 10,000 rebels had been killed, 9,000 captured and imprisoned, and 128—including Saya San himself and two of his closest associates, Saya Nyan and a hermit called Bandaka—had been hanged. Saya San went to the gallows with his head held high on 28 November 1931. On the Government side there had been no more than 50 casualties, including civil police and officials.

The death sentences were passed by a special tribunal set up by the Government to try the rebels. Trials were held in districts where insurrections had occurred, and many nationalistic lawyers eagerly volunteered to defend the accused, most of whom were ordinary, illiterate villagers. But one young pleader stood out among all these lawyers: Maung Saw, a native of Tharrawaddy and an ardent admirer of Saya San. He quickly ascended to prominence following his part in the trial, and the publication of a pamphlet in the form of an open letter to the British Secretary of State. To uphold the glory of Saya San *galons*, Maung Saw—who became U Saw when he got older—in 1938 raised his own force, named after Saya San's motley band of peasant rebels. Its personnel wore a green uniform and carried bamboo staves: the new *Galon Tat* had been born.

The abortive peasant revolt left the colonial victors jubilant in their clubs all over Burma: they ridiculed the naivety of the superstitious rebels, their hocus-pocus and gloated over how easy it had been to defeat them. But to the young intelligentsia in Rangoon and elsewhere, the Saya San rebellion provided an invaluable lesson in the art of guerrilla warfare. The hostilities were far from over; the confident colonial authorities could not have foreseen that just ten years later the tables would be turned.

Even as the peasant rebels were being slaughtered, serious-minded youths had begun discussing how to organise armed resistance against the British. These young men came from the national schools, which had been established after the 1920 student strike, and the so-called Anglo-vernacular schools, which were run by the Government and also used Burmese as the medium of instruction. Many of these students already had a sound knowledge of Burmese history and literature as well as Buddhism, more so than those who were being educated at exclusively European-code schools.

One such notable student was Ko Nu, or *kogyi* ("elder brother"), as he was known, who had graduated with a Bachelor of Arts degree from Rangoon University in 1929. Before returning to the university five years later, he had worked as Superintendent of the National Schools in Pantanaw town, where one of his colleagues was U Thant, future Secretary-General of the United Nations. It was during that academic year—1934–5—that Ko Nu met another ardently nationalistic student, Aung San, who was eight years his junior.

More students began to meet regularly to discuss politics, and before long an informal group had emerged at Rangoon University. Apart from Nu and Aung San, it also included Kyaw Nyein, a young man from Pyinmana in the central plains; Thein Pe, a good-looking, bespectacled intellectual who was well-read in Marxist literature; and M. A. Raschid, a Burmese Muslim of Subcontinental origin. All five of them were elected to the executive committee of the Rangoon University Students' Union for the year 1935–6. Nu became the chairman and Raschid vice-chairman. Aung San was appointed editor of the Union magazine, called *Oway* after the cry of the peacock, Burma's national symbol.

This young quintet were to lead the second student strike in Burma, which broke out in February 1936. Nu had been suspended for making critical speeches, and shortly afterwards Aung San was also expelled for refusing to reveal the name of the author of an article that had appeared in the *Oway* magazine. Entitled "Hellhound at Large", the article had ridiculed the university authorities. More than 700 students from Rangoon University and a few hundred from Judson College launched a strike to demand the re-admission of those who had been expelled. The strike soon spread to the Intermediate College in Mandalay and to high schools across the country. Only the European-code schools, whose pupils were generally more pro-British, did not support the mass movement that was brewing in Burma at that time.

Eventually, Nu and Aung San were readmitted, but that did not end the confrontation. As a result of the nation-wide character of the strike, an All-Burma Students' Union (ABSU) was set up with Raschid as its first president and Aung San as his vice. The students also reached out to other segments of society outside the secluded university campuses: the *Dohbama Asiayone* ("Our Burma Association") was founded under the auspices of Kodaw Hmaing, a respected writer and nationalist who had added the title "Thakin" to his name; *thakin* in Burmese, like *sahib* in Hindi, means master, and the Burmese were required to use it when addressing an Englishman. By calling himself "Thakin", Kodaw Hmaing wanted to demonstrate that he and other Burmese were "masters" of their country, not the British.

The first test of the strength and organisation of this broader, nation-wide movement came in 1937, when labour disputes broke out in central Burma's oilfields. The *Dohbama Asiayone* got involved and several young *thakins* travelled upcountry from Rangoon to assist the strikers. The workers decided to march on Rangoon to press their demands. The massive march towards the capital, which began in February 1938, went through the countryside, where the farmers showed sympathy and gave the workers food and shelter.

In the first week of December, the marchers were halted at the town of Magwe in the central Burmese plain. The police arrested the leaders and the rest were detained in a camp by the roadside. The workers went on a fast, and student leaders from Rangoon hurried up to reinforce them, as their leaders had been taken away. They too were arrested. The workers tried to continue their march, braving police truncheon charges and defying threats to shoot them if they went on. In the capital itself, large numbers of students picketed the Government's Secretariat office complex. The police were mobilised to crush the increasingly defiant protesters.

The students surrounding the Secretariat moved away at about noon on 20 December and assembled at the junction of Sparks and Fraser Streets to hear their leaders speak. Mounted police charged the crowd, wielding their truncheons. Police on foot lashed out with their *lathis*, or bamboo sticks. The young girls and high school pupils who were marching in front of the others took the first blows. A young student of Judson College, Ko Aung Gyaw, was beaten unconscious and died in hospital shortly afterwards.

The clash took place almost in front of the *Thuriya* ("the *Sun*") newspaper press, of which U Saw was the largest shareholder. His staff, and those of many other Burmese newspapers photographed the picketing and the police action, only to have their offices raided that night. Film and other documentary material were confiscated—later, however, the photographs were used as evidence before a special committee of enquiry that was set up to look into the incident.

Ko Aung Gyaw was accorded a hero's funeral on 27 December, attended by over 300,000 mourners. The title "Bo" ("officer" or "leader") was conferred upon him, and Sparks Street, where he was mortally wounded, was much later named after him. His grave, in the Kyandaw cemetery, was the first destination of the leaders of the army of oil-field workers and peasants who eventually reached the capital on 8 January 1939. Streams of marchers also entered Rangoon: the confluence was at the junction of Insein and Prome Roads, the northern gateway to the capital, where the Kamayut police station stands today.

The first groups of strikers and demonstrators numbered about 4,000, and they were joined by another 2,000 people from Rangoon who had come out to greet them. The 6,000-strong crowd, with a marching band in front, entered the capital. After paying their respects to Bo Aung Gyaw, who had fallen only twelve days before, they marched into Rangoon and halted on the slopes of the Shwe Dagon pagoda. Meetings were held and speeches made by representatives from both the *Dohbama Asiayone* and U Saw's *Galon Tat*.

Scores of people were arrested in the aftermath of the march on Rangoon. In fact, so many were rounded up that the Rangoon and Insein jails had to evacuate their convicts to make room for arrested protesters. But as a direct result of the movement, the All Burma Peasants Organisation and the All Burma Trades Union Congress were set up. US historian Frank Trager summed up the outcome of the movement of 1939 in these words:

> In brief, the Thakins succeeded in doing what the preceding generation of nationalist leaders had failed to do: they brought together, organised, and led a mass base of workers and peasants. They felt themselves to be an integral part of this group, and were its articulate spokesmen.

However, with the movement subdued, at least for the time being, in Rangoon, its centre of gravity shifted to Mandalay, the old Royal Capital. Large numbers of Buddhist monks had joined the protests there. Some 40,000-strong, they were a formidable force, and their participation added to the indigenous character of the ideas and methods which were deployed in the struggle against the colonial authorities.

On 10 February, mass meetings were held in Mandalay to protest against the arrests of several senior monks as well as local student leaders. A crowd of 50,000 people gathered outside the Eindawya Pagoda to listen to nationalist appeals. At 1 p.m., the crowd began moving towards the city centre, preceded by monks waving flags. Suddenly they discovered that armed policemen were blocking their way, with the British Deputy Commissioner himself in charge. The monks in the lead appealed to him to confer with their principal *sayadaw*, who was still busy organising more people at the starting point of the march. The Deputy Commissioner refused to heed the appeal; instead, regular troops took over from the police.

Eight ethnic Kachin soldiers from the Burma Rifles formed a firing position, with four standing up and four kneeling on the ground. They aimed their rifles, loaded with live ammunition. An officer advanced and gave the crowd a warning. Then a bugle was sounded—and the soldiers opened fire. Four shots were fired, and some monks in the vanguard of the procession fell to the ground. The people ran for their lives as the soldiers took aim again: a fusillade of bullets tore through the retreating demonstrators. When the carnage was over, dead and wounded lay on the ground, blood flowing copiously out on to the dusty street: 17 were dead, including seven monks, and 13 had been seriously injured.

A week later, on 17 February, hundreds of thousands of shocked and lamenting people from Mandalay as well as from the surrounding countryside attended the funeral of the 17 victims, who were laid to rest at the *Arzani* ("martyrs") Mausoleum, five miles south of the city on Amarapura Road.

The day before the funeral in Mandalay, the cabinet in Rangoon had lost a no-confidence motion in the House of Representatives. Burma's first Prime Minister, Dr. Ba Maw, the leader of the *Sinyetha Wunthanu* ("Nation Nationalist Proletarian") Party and the first prominent defender of Saya San's *galon* rebels, had been sworn in on 1 April 1937, and he was now, only two years later, forced to resign. He was succeeded by U Pu, a GCBA veteran from Tharrawaddy, who took over at a time when not only Burma but the entire world was in turmoil, with fascist powers emerging in the West as well as in the East.

Hitler invaded Poland on 1 September, and Great Britain and France declared war on Germany two days later. The Second World War had broken out. For Burma, this was a major turning point. U Pu rose in the House of Representatives in Rangoon, recommending that Burma should uphold Britain. Six months later, the House passed a resolution demanding that any aid to Britain's war effort should be conditional upon a promise by the colonial rulers of Dominion status within the Commonwealth. U Pu responded coolly to this popular demand, which led to his downfall in September 1940.

The *Dohbama Asiayone* and the students' unions went even further in their demands. They called for the cessation of all repressive measures by the colonial authorities and the immediate implementation of full democracy in Burma by the introduction of a constituent assembly elected by universal franchise, instead of the existing partly elected, partly appointed legislature.

The conflicts between various factions were further exacerbated when U Saw, who had served as Minister for Forests in U Pu's cabinet, became the new Prime Minister. U Saw's rise to power reflected his ambitious personality. He had won a seat on an alliance-ticket in the general elections in November 1936, but soon after joining U Pu's cabinet three years later, he came to realise that the Premier was losing popularity. Just as a no-confidence motion was tabled in August 1940, U Saw resigned from the government and voted against U Pu, thus tilting the balance and causing the government's downfall.

As Prime Minister, U Saw embarked on an authoritarian policy of systematically suppressing the opposition by taking advantage of the Defence of Burma Rules, a newly introduced war-time law that gave the government almost dictatorial powers. The *Dohbama Asiayone* movement was declared illegal and almost all U Saw's political rivals, including many prominent *thakins*, were arrested and charged with sedition, among them Thakin Nu, Thakin Soe, and Thakin Ba Sein, in addition to Dr. Ba Maw and Dr. Thein Maung, who were suspected of having links with the Japanese. At the same time, U Saw toured the countryside, eager to lay the ground-work for his popularity at the grassroots level. All those who manifested their loyalty to him were handsomely rewarded with key political and governmental positions.

His connections with higher authorities were cemented when the Governor, Sir Archibald Cochrane, left in 1941 and was succeeded by Sir Reginald Dorman-Smith. At only 42, Sir Reginald was about a year older than U Saw, and the two developed a lasting friendship. Sir Reginald had U Saw's tenure as Prime Minister extended for a further five-year term by postponing the general elections which should have been held in 1941. U Saw was subsequently invited to London for talks with Sir Winston Churchill and other British leaders: U Saw's purpose was to persuade them to "declare full independence for Burma after victory" in the Second World War. He was obsessed with power and wanted to secure his role in history as the liberator of Burma.

Before starting out on his journey to the West, U Saw, a professed Buddhist, paid his respects to the sacred Shwe Dagon. True to his maverick ways, he performed his obeisance from the sky: he flew around the 326- foot golden stupa in a Tiger Moth aeroplane. Most Buddhists must have considered the *galon* Prime Minister's curious act a sign of megalomania and profanity, as the stupa enshrines eight hairs of the Buddha and other sacred relics, which have to be kept higher than any mortal being.

Nevertheless, U Saw set off for London in early October 1941 together with U Tin Tut, the Cambridge-educated Vice-Chancellor of Rangoon University and a member of the prestigious Indian Civil Service.

A few months before U Saw staged his grandiose exit for London to ask for Dominion status, Thakin Aung San, unbeknownst to the Premier, had left by ship for Japan together with like-minded militant nationalists who at this time saw little hope in negotiating with the colonial power. The younger generation of nationalists had decided to fight for complete independence from Britain, without the links to the Crown that Dominion status involved. And they were convinced that this goal could be achieved only through an armed uprising.

Aung San was only in his mid-twenties but already a political veteran. He had served as the General Secretary of the *Dohbama Asiayone* and he was also the founder of the Freedom Bloc, a broader alliance, of which Dr. Ba Maw was the president—and they looked to the East rather than the West for help. In March 1940, after serving 17 days in prison, Aung San represented the Burmese nationalists at a meeting of the Indian National Congress at Ramgarh in India. There he met for the first time the urbane, sophisticated statesman Jawaharlal Nehru and also the much more hot-blooded Bengali nationalist, Subhas Chandra Bose. It is plausible to assume that Aung San was more impressed by the latter than the former.

On his return to Burma, Aung San discovered that the colonial authorities there had issued a warrant for his arrest. He decided to slip out of the country undetected. Together with a close friend, Thakin Hla Myaing,[1] he stowed away on a Chinese ship in Rangoon port with 200 Rupees in his pocket and a dream. He wanted to fight for Burma's independence and he had been instructed by other militant *thakins* to go to Shanghai to contact Mao communists. But he was in a hurry—the District Superintendent of Police, Henzada, a man called Xavier, had publicly advertised a reward of only 5 Rupees to turn Aung San in—so he and Hla Myaing took the first Chinese ship they could find. They disguised themselves as Chinese deck passengers Tan Luan Shung and Tan Su Taung.

It was 8 August 1940, and the ship happened to be destined for Amoy—a coastal Chinese city which was occupied by the Japanese, and now known as Xiamen. The Japanese tracked them down, and instead of ending up with Mao Zedong's partisans in the mountains of China, Aung San and Hla Myaing were taken to Tokyo. The Japanese listened carefully to the two young Burmese. They were promised what they wanted: arms and military training to fight the British. The Japanese took them to Thailand and, while Hla Myaing remained behind in Bangkok, Aung San, again in disguise, returned to Rangoon in February 1941.

The following month, he left with four of his comrades. Among them was his close friend Thakin Hla Pe (later known as Bo Let Ya) and Thakin Tun Shein, who later became Bo Yan Naing and married Dr. Ba Maw's daughter. With the cooperation of the Daitoa Shipping Company—one of many fronts for Japanese intelligence—they boarded the *Shunten Maru*, bound for Tokyo.

Military training began in April with just the six of them: Hla Myaing had returned from Bangkok to join the military exercises, which were held not in Japan proper but on the Japanese-held Chinese island of Hainan. In April, seven more young *thakins* were smuggled out of Burma by the Japanese on board a ship called the *Kairu Maru*. This batch included Ko Aung Thein and Thakin Shwe, who were later to be known under their *noms de guerre* Bo Ye Htut and Bo Kyaw Zaw. In early June, three more *thakins* followed, and in July two arrived in Hainan. A Burmese drama student in Tokyo, Ko Saung, had been present at the initial meeting but never participated in the actual military training in Hainan. But including him, there were now 19 young Burmese nationalists waiting to go back and fight for independence.

Then, in July, an unexpected fourth batch of eleven arrived on board the *Koreyu Maru*, which belonged to the same Japanese shipping line. This last group included several members of a minority faction of the *Dohbama Asiayone,* the so-called Thakin Ba Sein–Thakin Tun Oke group. Thakin Tun Oke himself was in this last batch, accompanied by Thakin Shu Maung, who had dropped out of Judson College in 1931 to work as a clerk in a suburban Rangoon post office (he was later to become Bo Ne Win). Their arrival caused some concern among Aung San and his comrades, who belonged to the majority *Dohbama Asiayone* faction, which honoured the old nationalist writer Thakin Kodaw Hmaing.

Frictions soon arose between the original group and the late-comers. According to Bo Kyaw Zaw, as quoted in Bertil Lintner's *Outrage: Burma's Struggle for Democracy*:

Aung San and Ne Win quarrelled quite often [in Hainan] .... Aung San was always very straight-forward; Ne Win much more cunning and calculating. But Aung San's main objection to Ne Win was his immoral character. He was a gambler and a womaniser, which the strict moralist Aung San—and the rest of us as well—despised. But for the sake of unity, we kept together as much we could.

But it should also be noted, as Bertil Lintner writes in his book:

The connection with Japan was not established simply because Aung San had caught the wrong ship in Rangoon. Japan's secret activities in Burma were undertaken by various agents in Rangoon and elsewhere. As early as the 1930s a Japanese naval officer called Shozo Kokubu had made contact with the Ba Sein-Tun Oke faction. In 1940 another nationalist, Dr. Thein Maung, had visited Tokyo on a trip arranged by a Japanese agent in Rangoon, Dr. Tsukasa Suzuki. Thakin Kodaw Hmaing's followers, including Aung San, were suspicious of the Japanese, and the aborted trip to China should be seen as an attempt to find another source of support for the struggle for independence. When that failed, only the Japanese option was open to the young Burmese nationalists.

The Japanese were clearly aware of this, which may help explain why they decided to include the extreme right-wing, Axis-oriented Tun Oke-Ba Sein faction in their training programme. Thakin Ba Sein, the actual founder of the *Dohbama Asiayone*, had together with Thakin Tun Oke begun contacting the Japanese as early as 1938. On their recommendation, Ba Sein had already tried to cross the border to Thailand in October 1940, only to be caught and imprisoned.

Whatever the case, with the arrival of the last batch, these were altogether 30 young nationalists. Hence, they became known in Burmese history as "The Thirty Comrades". Their Japanese commander was Col. Keiji Suzuki, the officer who had apprehended Aung San and Hla Myaing in Amoy. While the only guiding principle of at least the Thakin Kodaw Hmaing faction of the Thirty Comrades was freedom for Burma, Col. Suzuki and Japanese intelligence clearly had other motives.

The Japanese had invaded northern and eastern China in 1938, and the Allies were supporting the Kuomintang effort to resist the Imperial Army's advance west, towards the Chinese interior and ultimately India. Tons of war material were funnelled into the southwestern Chinese province of Yunnan, a stronghold of Chiang Kai-shek's Kuomintang forces. The Burma Road from the port of Rangoon, across the sun-baked plains of central Burma into the Shan hills and on to

Yunnan was the main supply line. The Japanese wanted to cut this line of communication by invading Burma. In order to do so, the Japanese wanted an indigenous Burmese fighting force that could make the operation successful. This intelligence programme was code-named the *Minami Kikan*, and the young Burmese in Japan formed a vital part of it.

In December, 28 of the 30 comrades were transferred to Bangkok; Ko Saung never joined the army and one of the young Burmese, Thakin Than Tin, had succumbed to malaria in Formosa, to where the training had shifted after the initial exercises in Hainan. The Burma Independence Army (BIA) was formally set up in Bangkok on the 26th. Thakin Hla Pe later recalled:

> Enthusiasm ran high and each one of us drew blood from the arm to drink an oath of loyalty. That night we had a meeting of all those who had returned from the training camps in Japan, and Aung San suggested that we should each pick an auspicious name that would give us pride and confidence and sense of mission, a name to carry on our march. It was Aung San's idea and not one that we conceived by collective or prolonged thinking. We liked the idea when it was put to us, and at the meeting we made our selections, tried them out, liked them, and felt a few inches taller wearing the new names.

"Bo" was added to all their new *noms de guerre*: it was a military title that commanded respect and authority. Thus, Aung San became Bo Teza ("Powerful"), Hla Pe assumed the name Bo Let Ya ("Right-Hand Man"), Thakin Aung Than was Bo Setkya ("the Flying Weapon"), Shu Maung became Bo Ne Win ("Bright Sun") and so on. The sole exception was Thakin Tun Oke, who assumed a Japanese name. Col. Suzuki, the commander of the group, was named Bo Mogyo ("Thunder"). The Japanese officer had also wanted a Burmese name, and his *nom de guerre* was given to him by Aung San himself. But apart from the literal meaning of thunder, there was a much more subtle explanation for Suzuki's Burmese name. A Burmese saying circulated during British rule: *htiyo-ko mogyo pyit mai*. This prophecy literally meant, "a Royal Dynasty [the British Raj] will be struck by a bolt of lightning". Japanese Bo Mogyo took command of the BIA Headquarters with the rank and title of General Minami (Col. Suzuki), with Major-Gen. Murakami (Capt. Noda) as Chief of Staff. Major Gen. Omoda (Aung San) was appointed Senior Staff Officer (the most senior Burmese). Eight other Burmese officers, holding the ranks of lieutenant-colonels to captains, were appointed to HQ and various other detachments. Ne Win's posting appeared at the bottom of the list. He was given command of the Squad Directing Harassing Forces Within Burma with the title, Lt. Col. Shu Maung. His talents were obviously suited to that task.

In early 1942, the BIA entered Burma together with the Japanese army. Apart from the initial 28, many more Burmese joined in Thailand and along the actual border. The proud standards[2] they held high as they marched forward on their native soil were tricolour topped by a yellow line expressing the religious faith, the green in the middle denoted the country's lush land and its agricultural pursuits, and the red below—intrepidity. In the centre, is a circle with a white background, the peacock of Burma in its pride was displayed, symbolising honour, dignity and glory of the nation. They numbered about 2,300 in the beginning and soon swelled to 30,000 by the time they reached central Burma. On 7 March 1942, Rangoon was captured by the Japanese, aided by the BIA. The British retreated to India in the west.

The myth of European invincibility had been dispelled. But the realities of Japanese occupation were no less brutal, as the Burmese nationalists soon discovered to their dismay.

The dreaded Japanese *Kempetai* intelligence machine was well trained in torture of anyone suspected of being a "spy", without discriminating between friend and foe. Asians suffered as much as captured Europeans, as the infamous "Death Railway" from Thailand to Burma clearly shows.

Dr. Ba Maw was proclaimed Head of State, or *Naingandaw Adipadi* ("Supreme Ruler") when the Japanese finally granted Burma "independence" on 1 August 1943. But the rest of the Thirty Comrades were disgusted. Thakin Thein Pe was sent to India and made contact with the Allied High Command in Calcutta. On 27 March 1945, the Burmese nationalist forces—now renamed the Patriotic Burmese Forces—turned their guns against the Japanese. Allied forces in India pushed east, and at the beginning of May, the Japanese were forced to retreat from Rangoon.

The British were back, but so too was the Burmese nationalist movement. Renewed rallies were held in Rangoon to press demands for complete independence for Burma. Sir Reginald Dorman-Smith, the British Governor who had spent the war years in exile in Simla, India, returned on 16 October 1945. But well before that, on 19 August, the nationalists—now reorganised as the Anti-Fascist People's Freedom League (AFPFL), led by Aung San—had held a mass meeting in the Nethurein Cinema Hall in Rangoon, demanding full independence for Burma, outside the Commonwealth.

However, the former forces of the war-time resistance had meanwhile been disarmed, save for a few battalions, which were allowed to become part of the post-war Burma Army according to an agreement reached between the British and the Burmese nationalists in Kandy, Ceylon (now Sri Lanka), in September 1945. Those who refused to surrender their weapons on 1 December formed the People's Volunteer Organisation (PVO), which became in effect a militia force loyal to Aung San.

From then on, events moved quickly. U Saw never served the full extra five years that Sir Reginald had given him as Prime Minister. He had been away on his visit to England when Burma had been invaded by the Japanese, and upon hearing of their advance in East Asia, he had tried to contact Tokyo's ambassador in Lisbon, Portugal. He was subsequently arrested by the British and interned by the colonial authorities in Uganda, East Africa, from 1942 to the end of the war. On his return to Burma, he reformed his *Myochit* Party and rebuilt his paramilitary force, the *Galon Tat*, which was ready to restart its scramble for power in Rangoon.

In December 1946, Britain's new Labour Prime Minister, Clement Attlee, invited Aung San and other AFPFL leaders to talks in London to discuss Burma's future. "We want complete independence. There is no question of dominion status for Burma", Aung San said in New Delhi on his way to London in January 1947. But in an attempt to forge national unity, other Burmese political leaders were also included in Aung San's London delegation.

The "opposition" was represented by the disgraced U Saw—who had lost out to Aung San during the war—and Thakin Ba Sein, another opponent of Aung San. When an agreement to grant Burma independence was reached on 27 January, both U Saw and Ba Sein refused to sign. But the agreement was reached, Burma was going to become an independent republic outside the Commonwealth. Clement Attlee himself, however, later claimed that Aung San's attitude towards the British had mellowed during his visit to London:

> They [the Burmese delegation] had, unfortunately, committed themselves to their followers in favour of complete independence and a Republic...as the talks proceeded, their distrust disappeared and I think some of them—particularly their leader, Aung San, a strong character, began to realise the desirability of remaining in the Commonwealth.

One of the members of the youthful Burmese delegation to London had apparently stated during the discussion: "We're just a lot of raw lads."

Most noteworthy, however, was Clement Attlee's assessment of U Saw. Paraphrasing William Shakespeare, he concluded:

> They were a very pleasant lot, except for one representative of the minority Party—U Saw. I had met him before the war ended. I came to regard him as a man who would "smile and smile and be a villain".

3

The Trial

When the trial of U Saw and his accomplices was about to begin a few months after the assassination, Sir Hubert Rance, the British Governor at the time and destined to be the last, encountered some unexpected difficulties in appointing a special tribunal to try the gang. The selection of Justice Kyaw Myint of the High Court as the President went smoothly enough, but when it came to appointing two suitable members from among other senior lawmen, the task suddenly became much more difficult. Several of the nominees appeared reluctant to take on the duty. Some excused themselves as having "heart problems", while a few refused outright to serve with the tribunal. However, eventually two senior Sessions Judges, U Aung Tha Gyaw and U Si Bu, accepted, and Sir Hubert inaugurated the three-man Special Tribunal on 20 September 1947.

The first meeting was held four days later, when the prosecution's complaint was heard and the examination of the King's witnesses began. The trial itself was delayed until 15 October, to allow U Saw to secure the legal services of Mr. Benjamin Raphael Vertannes, a former Pleader in the Rangoon High Court, who was now living in England.

When the trial eventually commenced, at the court of the Special Tribunal in Insein, it was the King versus:

1. U Saw, alleged ringleader
2. Maung Soe, alleged assassin
3. Thet Hnin, alleged assassin
4. Maung Sein, *aka* Sein Gyi, *aka* Hla Aung, alleged assassin
5. Yan Gyi Aung, *aka* Hla Tun, alleged assassin
6. Thu Kha, alleged driver of the vehicle that brought the assassins to the Secretariat
7. Khin Maung Yin, alleged accomplice
8. Maung Ni, *aka* Bo Ni, *aka* Gani, alleged accomplice
9. Hmon Gyi, *aka* Maung Hmon, alleged accomplice

There had been nine martyrs, and now nine men stood accused of their murder. The only man conspicuous by his absence from the dock was Ba Nyunt, one of the occupants of the Fordson truck, who had gone ahead to reconnoitre the Secretariat before the arrival of the gunmen. To the surprise of many—and to the consternation of U Saw—Ba Nyunt had agreed to act as witness against the rest of the gang. He had attended an Anglo-vernacular high school, and thus was the best educated of U Saw's hitmen. Presumably, he understood more of the national and historical implications of the crime than the other rougher and more trigger-happy members of U Saw's *Galon Tat*. There was a carrot as well: Ba Nyunt was granted a conditional pardon in exchange for turning King's evidence.

It was a public trial, held in a room within the Insein Jail, and tickets had to be obtained for the sessions because of limited seating and the great demand to witness the proceedings. People were jostling to get tickets; the spectacle that unfolded was a mixture of British justice and a drama performance in the best Burmese tradition.

U Saw appeared daily in the courtroom, cool, calm, and collected. He was well dressed in traditional Burmese silk attire, as befitting a former Prime Minister. He could not be described as handsome, yet he exuded an air of mystique which had a certain appeal, especially to the ladies, who occupied a good number of seats in the hall. His dress, however, was not entirely formal, as he did not wear the usually obligatory *gaung-baung*, a kind of turban worn by Burmese males on official occasions. In fact, his close-cropped hair made him look almost nondescript, like any other peasant from his native Tharrawaddy district in rustic, lower Burma.

Every now and then, U Saw looked over at his accomplices in a fatherly way; after all, they had been his loyal followers for years. But even before the assassination was carried out all his men had to take an oath of fidelity, after which they had to sign a note—some of them called it a *thaydansa* (a will)—stating that they were to die because of their own acts since they had betrayed their country. Ba Nyunt had been the first to give in to the pressure, and he had been lavishly rewarded: his life was to be spared if he agreed to tell the Tribunal everything he knew. And so he did.

Ba Nyunt first revealed that a meeting had been held at U Saw's Ady Road residence on 18 July—the very night before the assassination. Ba Nyunt stated that he knew nothing about the plot before this briefing; he had just returned from a long journey and was already asleep when he was woken up suddenly and summoned to an urgent audience with the boss U Saw. Maung Soe, Thet Hnin,

Maung Sein, and Thu Kha were already seated in front of the paramount chief of the *Galon Tat* when Ba Nyunt presented himself at 9 p.m.

As he sat down, U Saw calmly informed him that these four men had been assigned to eliminate the entire Executive Council, specially targeting Aung San. Ba Nyunt gaped in disbelief. He was even more stunned when U Saw told him that his personal task was to kill Thakin Nu, Speaker of the Constituent Assembly. Ba Nyunt nodded, more out of respect for his boss than in approval of the ghastly scheme; there was, of course, no way he could question his boss's order or in any other way challenge the assignment.

Before this astonishing night-time meeting at U Saw's residence, Ba Nyunt and his team had been engaged in collecting arms and ammunition from various sources. They had hidden them in concealed containers in Inya Lake behind U Saw's house, or transported them to the chief's home town, Tharrawaddy. Shooting lessons had been given on Cabin Island in the lake, Ba Nyunt revealed; they had also practised by firing at trees inside U Saw's Ady Road residential compound. "But we thought it was all meant for a bank robbery," Ba Nyunt said. "I had no idea that the plan was to wipe out the cabinet until that night before the assassination."

Although Ba Nyunt turned out to be the most important witness to appear before the Tribunal, he was by no means the only person testifying against U Saw. After the carnage in the Secretariat on the 19th, more than 800 people were rounded up all over Rangoon. Most of them were released after interrogation by the CID, the Insein police, and the Rangoon City Police. Finally, out of 131 witnesses filed by the prosecution, 78 appeared for the King. Among them were several witnesses to the actual attack inside the Secretariat: Htin Baw the clerk; the young peon Thaung Sein, who had guarded the door; the journalist Maung Than, who witnessed the murder of Ko Htwe; and Sein Maung, the diligent reporter who had jotted down the number of the jeep in which the assassins escaped. All testified before the Tribunal.

Tun Hla Oung also ordered a more thorough search of U Saw's Ady Road residence. Eight cases of .303 ammunition, four Tommy guns, and a Sten gun were found in the lake behind the house, where U Saw had built a family shrine. The captured weapons were inspected by a ballistics expert, who also examined spent bullets from the bodies of the victims. The investigator reached the conclusion that four of the five guns retrieved from the lake "were used by the assassins against their victims in the Secretariat on 19 July".

Two false number plates made of metal were also found: one plate read RC 1814, the number noted on the assassins' jeep, and the other RA 3123, presumably used by the Fordson truck. The former had yellow paint on the other side and the number RB 4140. When my father had arrived at U Saw's residence in the afternoon of 19 July, he had found a Fordson truck bearing the number plate MTLA 183 and two jeeps numbered RB 9831 (the hooded one with the paint still wet) and Gen. 167 (the vehicle that did not start). The police managed to trace the actual RB 9831 number to a jeep registered in the name of one U Ba Aye of Zalun Street in Sanchaung, another northern Rangoon suburb. Ba Nyunt revealed that Khin Maung Yin, one of his companions in the Fordson truck, who was also the nephew of U Saw's wife Daw Than Khin, had been given the task of painting the number plates.

Further searches in the lake behind U Saw's house led to a major, even more intriguing discovery. About ten metres from the bank, packed in air-tight tins and quite dry, were 37 Bren guns, 59 spare barrels, eight fully loaded .38 revolvers, one Colt pistol, three US-made carbines, five Tommy guns with six magazines, three Sten guns, two jerrycans filled with approximately 7,000 rounds of Sten ammunition, three .303 rifles with 7,000 rounds of ammunition in clips, 15 cases with more .303 bullets, 30 bandoliers each with 50 rounds of .303 ammunition, and 75 Mark-36 British Mills hand grenades.

In another house in Rangoon, whose owner was connected with U Saw's *Galon Tat*, the police discovered 44 hand grenades, 49 detonators, 730 rounds of .303 ammunition, 3,000 rounds of Sten ammunition, seven cases of armour-piercing cartridges and time switches, seven cases of hand grenades as well as magazines for Brens, Tommy guns, and carbines. U Saw and his henchmen had enough military hardware to stage a revolution in Rangoon—which indeed may have been the plan. What were U Saw and his men actually up to? Nobody knew; not even Ba Nyunt was able to provide any more clues.

The court proceedings continued for weeks, with people still queuing up outside every morning to get tickets for the day's performance. The evidence against U Saw was mounting even further. When a number of important witnesses had been examined, charges could be brought against all nine of them: conspiracy to murder, abetment to murder, and "the commission of murder in furtherance of common intention", as the full legal expression described U Saw's own involvement in the plot.

Strangely, however, the evidence—and the changed attitude of his erstwhile follower Ba Nyunt—did not seem to deter U Saw. Neither did he appear ruffled with the confessions of his other men. Instead, by mid-November, U Saw decided to seek further legal assistance. With the help of his brother U Maung Maung Ji, who lived in England, a renowned King's Counsel, Frederick Henry Curtis-Bennett, was hired. Although U Saw was reputed to be a wealthy man, he had to deposit his family jewels as surety in banks to obtain quick loans to cover these extra expenses.

When Curtis-Bennett finally arrived at the gates of Insein Jail on 8 December to meet U Saw for the first time, my father-in-law, Justice Thaung Sein, was there to greet him. The British lawyer was duly informed that, as a matter of routine, he would have to be searched. Curtis-Bennett agreed and was in return granted the right to visit his client freely. His wallet was, however, handed over to the prison staff. It was sealed and kept in the prison's safe. While this was happening, U Saw heard that his British lawyer was being "harassed", and he objected vehemently. U Saw was pacified only when Curtis-Bennett entered the court room and explained the circumstances.

The British Counsel's legal strategy soon became evident. In order to prove his client's innocence he shifted the entire blame for conspiracy and abetment to murder on to the Approver Ba Nyunt, whom he accused of being the main organiser of the plot to kill Aung San. U Saw, Curtis-Bennett went on, had been unaware of Ba Nyunt's schemes and knew nothing about the assassination until it had taken place. The British lawyer made an analogy with the fate that befell Thomas Becket, Archbishop of Canterbury, in 1170, when four of King Henry's men, acting on their own accord, killed the unfortunate priest in his own cathedral. The King's violent show of anger against Becket had caused his squires to commit the murder in an attempt to please their lord.

The lawyer further presented an "open house plea", whereby in having to allow free and easy access to supporters, politicians cannot be held accountable for acts committed by any of their crowds of visitors. To support his arguments, veteran politicians, among them Dr. Ba Maw and Thakin Ba Sein, were brought in as defence witnesses and cross-examined. Ba Sein had been taken into protective custody two days after the assassination, as both he and Dr. Ba Maw were organising an alliance to oppose the AFPFL and therefore could have had a hand in the plot. Their friendship with U Saw was well known, but they responded to the questions about their relationship by saying, as U Saw did, that as politicians they routinely met with supporters, followers, and fellow politicians. No firm link between U Saw and other leading politicians could be established.

But the prosecution simply rebutted Curtis-Bennett's rather odd comparison between the killing of the Archbishop of Canterbury and the mass murder of Burma's cabinet by stating that U Saw was not a king but a person perfectly capable of master-minding the crime of which he stood accused. The irony of the comparison with the murder of Thomas Becket was that King Henry was humiliated and the victim canonised, a point that Curtis-Bennett seemed to have missed.

Furthermore, there was actually precious little Curtis-Bennett could do to discredit Ba Nyunt's crucial testimony. The case against U Saw became even more solid when the prosecution presented its thirty-ninth witness: Captain H. Khan, U Saw's neighbour, who had almost crashed into the assassins' jeep on 19 July. As it turned out, Tun Hla Oung had already placed U Saw's house under surveillance on the 17th; U Saw's growing arrogance and the suspicion that he was hiding weapons in his compound had attracted the attention of the CID. The first to be assigned to watch U Saw's residence was Head Constable Aung Kyaw Sein—and he was followed by Capt. Khan on the 18th. Khan, in turn, had ordered two of his most reliable men, his clerk Hla Tin and another man called Soe Myint, to maintain a round-the-clock surveillance of the suspicious, fortress-like Ady Road compound on the peninsula in Inya Lake. One of Khan's men pretended he was a fisherman, which gave him an excellent excuse to spend hours sitting on the bank of the lake.

On the morning of the 19th, all three of them—Capt. Khan and his two men—had been keeping a watch on the compound from different vantage points opposite the peninsula. At 10 a.m., Hla Tin reported, almost routinely, back to Khan that a jeep had left U Saw's compound. Through his binoculars, Hla Tin had spotted four or five men in it wearing what looked like "raincoats". The jeep's number was noted as RC 1814. Hla Tin had also seen U Saw himself come to the gate to see the jeep off, then apparently whisper something to the man watching the entrance to the compound before walking back towards the house. An hour later, Khan almost collided with the very same jeep as it was returning from its mission.

Other, more intriguing details also came out during the trial. CID chief Tun Hla Oung was asked about the significance of the red and white pieces of cloth on the windscreen of the assassins' jeep. My father replied: "*Nats* [spirits] must be propitiated when people are about to undertake any dangerous enterprise, or go on a journey, to avert calamity that might befall them or their families." Hence, any onlookers probably realised that the jeep they saw speeding through Rangoon that day in July must have been on an extremely important mission.

But the merciful *nats* did not seem to be on U Saw's side when, following closely behind his lawyer, he came forward to give evidence under oath on 11 December. In his thirty years in politics, U Saw asserted, he had always been a firm believer in non-violence. It was out of the question that he would have approved of such a foolhardy and heinous crime as the plot perpetrated by Ba Nyunt and his fellow conspirators. Eyebrows were raised in the audience. U Saw had had his own private militia, the *Galon Tat*, and was certainly not known as any kind of Burmese Mahatma Gandhi. U Saw went on to claim that he had been sick with stomach pains on the afternoon of 18 July, and remained in bed for most of the following day as well. Someone had informed him about the assassination at about noon on the 19th, and that, he said, was the first time he heard about the tragic event.

His eight co-defendants, his close followers, responded half-heartedly to the charges. Only Maung Ni came forth to give evidence on oath. He pleaded not guilty and said he knew nothing about the plot. He just happened to be a passenger in the Fordson truck that day in July. Another occupant of the truck, Hmon Gyi, entered a simple plea of denial, as did three of the actual gunmen: Maung Soe, Thet Hnin, and Yan Gyi Aung.

Soon, however, U Saw's hitherto faithful followers began to give in, possibly in the hope of having their sentences reduced. The nephew of U Saw's wife, Khin Maung Yin, who had been in the first truck, stated that he had lived in their house since June 1942. He went on to testify that, given the difference in age, he had been obliged to obey U Saw.

Under questioning by the Tribunal, Khin Maung Yin broke down and admitted that he was familiar with the guns that had been seized in U Saw's compound and later exhibited during the trial. After similar confessions, the driver of the assassins' jeep, Thu Kha, and gunmen Maung Sein, Maung Ni, and Hmon Gyi submitted pleas of mitigation, saying they were only carrying out orders. Of those who had followed Ba Nyunt in confessing, only the teenager Yan Gyi Aung later retracted his statement, claiming police coercion. Approver Ba Nyunt had implicated all nine accused in the plot.

As motives were being sought for the crimes, it became increasingly evident that U Saw was more than just Aung San's political rival. On 21 September 1946, ten months before the carnage in the Secretariat, an attempt had been made on

U Saw's life. He had visited Government House, and left the building in the late afternoon to go home, with two of his men following in a car behind. When he reached a roundabout on Prome Road in Myenigon—on the way home to Ady Road—he looked back and noted a jeep coming up behind his vehicle.

When pulling uphill on the other side of the roundabout, U Saw's driver slowed down for a bad stretch of the road. The jeep had caught up to him and U Saw spotted four PVO militiamen in uniform and the muzzle of a weapon pointing at his car. A shot was fired, and the jeep sped away. The bullet had passed through both windows of U Saw's car. He was not hit, but was badly cut about the eyes by glass. One eye was in a serious condition and U Saw was hospitalised for a few days after the incident, and he had to briefly visit India to have his eye examined by a medical expert.

The assailants were never identified, but U Saw suspected that Aung San had been behind the attempt on his life; after all, he had noticed clearly that the men in the jeep were wearing PVO uniforms. This did not deter U Saw from accompanying Aung San to London in January 1947 to negotiate Burma's independence with Prime Minister Clement Attlee—but the wily Burmese politician had showed his disapproval of Aung San by refusing to sign the agreement with the British on the 27th.

Throughout the trial the Home Minister, U Kyaw Nyein, appeared worried about the way in which the prosecution appeared to hesitate to push forward with its evidence. He remarked on it several times, but the legal experts were more concerned about ensuring the fairness and professionalism of the historic trial. The CID chief, my father Tun Hla Oung, had completely encircled the pentagon-shaped Insein Jail complex with armed guards around the clock. A fully equipped intelligence unit manned the gates and U Saw's every move was watched. His request for daily visits by his wife was turned down, but an inmate serving a five-year sentence was closeted in the same cell as U Saw to cook and wait on him. According to Justice Thaung Sein: "We were concerned not only about U Saw's safety from attack by other inmates but also about rendering the prison impregnable from escape or rescue attempts."

These fears were not unjustified. An attempt to escape had already been uncovered during U Saw's first week of incarceration. And despite the strict security surrounding Insein Jail, U Saw's lavish lifestyle inside the prison soon caught the attention of many. In deference to his former status as Prime Minister, U Saw had been assigned a large cell consisting of four rooms interconnected by arches, where he stayed with his "butler", as he called his cook and servant. U Saw's first show of largesse had been to give a feast of fried noodles to the prison staff. He insisted on having a peg of whisky morning and night "for medical reasons", and easily polished off a bottle of whisky every two or three days.

The alacrity with which the Scotch was served, and the general laxity in guarding the important prisoner, also alarmed minister Kyaw Nyein, who requested the incumbent Inspector General of Prisons, Col. Ba Thaw, to step down. His post was taken over by Justice Thaung Sein, who also continued to serve as Secretary of the Judicial Affairs Ministry. The further tightening up of security also reflected concerns over the increasingly volatile political situation in the country outside the confines of Insein Jail.

But the trial continued, until finally, on 30 December, the Special Tribunal, after analysing the mass of accumulated evidence, submitted its 25,000-word judgment. Dr. Maung Maung, a Burmese lawyer and author, was in the crowd of legal experts, journalists and others who had gathered in the open court that day:

> The judgment ran over an hour of reading time. The courtroom was crowded again, as it was on the first day of the trial. The accused were present, eight men in the dock, U Saw seated in a chair beside his counsel. Reporters showed some restlessness and impatience as the delivery of the judgment rolled on, seemingly unending. Listening, I felt fascinated by the summing up of the case, and the tone of the delivery, soft, impeccable, impersonal, near yet so far away. The accused sat and listened, emotionless; many of them did not understand what was being said in English, and all of them probably felt relieved that it was over at last

> The four gunmen—Maung Soe, Thet Hnin, Yan Gyi Aung, and Maung Sein—were found guilty of murder, and U Saw, Thu Kha, Maung Ni, Hmon Gyi, and Khin Maung Yin of abetment to murder. They were all sentenced to death.

Since the entire judgment was in English, it is doubtful whether U Saw understood all that was being said. His education was rather rudimentary; that of his followers even more so. But they must have sensed the gravity of the punishment meted out to them through the tone of Justice Kyaw Myint's voice—and the reaction from the crowd in the courtroom. A few minutes elapsed before U Saw stood up. Questioned by the judge whether he understood the sentence, he replied in a low but firm voice: "Yes, I do."

His voice trembled as he endeavoured to plead that he had submitted certain evidence that should have been accepted, whereas other testimonies presented by the prosecution had been believed too easily.

U Saw sank down in his chair beside his counsel. When a police officer tried to handcuff him before taking him out of court, he snapped: "Why should I be handcuffed?" But he appeared more bewildered than arrogant as he glanced entreatingly at Justice Thaung Sein nearby. The trusted Justice intervened and allowed U Saw to be escorted out of the courtroom unmanacled. But he was taken to a cell reserved for people on death row, not the one he had occupied since his arrest on 19 July.

The convicted men had been warned by the Special Tribunal that appeals against their death sentences would have to be submitted within seven days of sentencing. That week would take them into a new judicial era in Burma, since the country was going to become an independent republic outside of the Commonwealth on 4 January 1948. The Supreme Court in Rangoon, not the Privy Council in London, would become the final court of appeal. His Majesty would be replaced by the Union of Burma, in other words, it would be "The State vs. U Saw and His Men".

The appeals of U Saw and the other convicted men were duly presented to the High Court. The appeals were dismissed. The High Court stated that each of the men "had a vital part to play in the conspiracy". No judicial reasons were found for interference with the sentences. The men then asked for leave to appeal to the Supreme Court, which considered their pleas—and eventually rejected them after seeking guidance from previous rulings by the Privy Council in London.

There was only one course left to the nine convicts. This last hope was to ask for mercy from the President. The first to hold that paramount honour of the new republic was Sao Shwe Thaike, the *sawbwa* (prince) of the Shan state of Yawnghwe. It was only in the final hours that three of the men had their sentences reduced to "transportation for life", which meant twenty years' imprisonment: Thu Kha, the jeep driver; Khin Maung Yin, whose duty had been confined to reconnoitring the Secretariat before the assassins arrived; and Maung Ni, the man who with a revolver guarded the exit for the getaway. The rest were to hang.

In a last resort to spare his young son's life, Yan Gyi Aung's father produced a horoscope for the members of the court in an attempt to prove that the boy was only 16 years old. No proper birth certificate existed, but a medical examiner decided that Yan Gyi Aung was at least 17. The Tribunal therefore fixed his birthdate as 1 January 1930. In this way, he would turn 18 before his execution was to take place later in 1948.

The bodies of Bogyoke Aung San and the other slain leaders were still lying in state at the Jubilee Hall on Shwe Dagon Pagoda Road in Rangoon when the Special Tribunal read out the judgment on 30 December 1947. The Jubilee Hall— a solid brick structure, ivy covered, ornate, and very English in appearance—was built as a theatre, with a stage at one end and a balcony, with two stairways on either side leading up to it, at the other. The spacious auditorium had gleaming teak floors and the surrounding gardens supplemented the covered space when exhibitions and public meetings were held.

Ironically, just two months before the assassination of Aung San and his colleagues, the Anti-Fascist People's Freedom League had held a general convention at this very hall as a prelude to the summoning of the Constituent Assembly, which was going to draft independent Burma's first constitution. Aung San himself had opened the convention on 19 May.

Aung San's body had been conveyed from his residence in Tower Lane to the Jubilee Hall the day after he was killed. He and five of the other martyrs lay in raised glass caskets on the floor of the auditorium; Sao Sam Htun's body had earlier been taken by road and rail to his home town in the Shan Hills. Abdul Razak and Ko Htwe had been buried according to Muslim rites.

The military and civil police, the three services of the armed forces—the army, the navy, and the air force—and militiamen of the People's Volunteer Organisation (PVO) took turns to stand guard as thousands came to pay their last respects to the fallen leaders. The head of each martyr was exposed and the pallor of their skin showed the grey marks of their wounds. Only a few who saw them could hold back their tears.

But security was tight as well. As each party of mourners completed their walk around the auditorium, they were asked to stand in line facing the caskets and, at a command, to bow. When they had walked out, another group was allowed to enter.

On 11 April 1948, the caskets were conveyed on their last journey from the Jubilee Hall, where they had lain in state for almost nine months, to a newly erected mausoleum north of the Shwe Dagon Pagoda. The funeral cortege wended its way up Shwe Dagon Pagoda Road, with the police and the regular army keeping order. The covered caskets, accompanied by a large framed portrait of the martyrs, were carried on open trucks and jeeps. More than 500,000 people followed the vehicles, moving slowly up towards the southern stairway of the Shwe Dagon. PVO militiamen, who had loved Aung San as their *bogyokegyi* and true leader, marched alongside the procession.

Completing an anti-clockwise half-circle around the golden pagoda, the cavalcade reached the new mausoleum. Soldiers and sailors shouldered the caskets and carried them into the new building. The PVOs must then have felt that it was their very last opportunity to serve their leaders; they took over the coffins and, in lowering them into the cavities, stood on top of the walls of the sepulchral chambers. Pieces of brick and fresh concrete fell from under their booted feet to the platform below. Finally, the bodies of the martyrs were laid to rest.

The crowds gradually mélted away, and the masons cleaned up after sealing the tombs. As darkness fell, even the raucous crows were silent.

4

The Mystery

Anthony Stonor, a young Briton serving with the 2nd Battalion of the Welch Regiment in Kalaw at the time of Aung San's assassination, was in the capital on duty on 14 September 1947. He entered the Officers' Club in Rangoon, which was situated on the first floor of a building on Sule Pagoda Road and boasted of having the longest bar in the Far East. At this time, it had the added attraction of a resident dance band, led by the brilliant Indian guitarist, Cedric West. Stonor and some other young officers from his battalion sat down and ordered drinks. They had not been at the famous bar long when the doors burst open and two Burmans rushed in. One of them, a burly man in his early thirties, began to shout: "U Saw didn't kill Aung San! I know it and so do you British, for you were behind it!" He and his companion then commenced to smash all the glasses and bottles behind the bar.

The most senior commander present was a colonel of the Gurkhas and he shouted to the rest of the astonished British officers: "Don't do anything! Ignore them! I'll send for the Military Police!" Stonor and his friends sat in silence while the two Burmans continued with their destruction. At a small table sitting by himself was a young and slender 2nd Lieutenant of the Gurkhas, who was sipping a glass of beer. The burly Burman walked across to him and knocked the glass out of his hand. The young officer jumped to his feet and with an upper-cut knocked the man over the table and flat on his back on the floor.

Stonor looked at his friends and asked in bewilderment: "Who's that man?" Another officer replied: "It's Thakin Than Tun, Aung San's brother-in-law."

At that moment, the Military Police arrived, picked up the half-stunned Than Tun and his friend and led them away. The barman started to sweep up the broken glass, while Cedric West and the band struck up the latest tune of the day. But the evening was spoilt for Stonor and his friends; they left and made their way to the Sun Café for a steak.

Rumours of British involvement in the assassination of Aung San were so persistent at the time that Thakin Nu's government had had to issue a firm denial as early as 25 July, less than a week after the tragedy:

Rumours connecting His Majesty's Government and His Excellency the Governor of Burma with the recent dastardly murders of the Hon'able U Aung San and others of the Executive Council, have spread into certain sections of the public. The Government of Burma wish it to be known that these rumours are utterly unfounded and that there is close understanding between His Majesty's Government, His Excellency the Governor and the Burma Government. They are actively co-operating with the view to bringing the culprits to book, with the least possible delay.

But the people were in an emotional state and the political situation was tense, which was one of the reasons why security at Insein Jail had to be tightened. "The mourning nation was like a chicken with its head cut off", Justice Thaung Sein recalled. Some sensational newspapers exploited the situation by publishing unsubstantiated allegations. On 28 July, three days after the Government's attempt to dispel the rumours, the *Rangoon Guide Daily*, ran a story which even prompted the Governor, Sir Hubert Rance, to send off an urgent telegram to the Earl of Listowel, Secretary of State for Burma at the Foreign Office in London. The story ran:

Last January [1947] when the Burma delegation, headed by Aung San, signed the Aung San-Attlee Agreement, U Saw and Thakin Ba Sein refused to sign, and U Saw remained behind when all the others returned. We [the *Guide Daily*] had already told the country that U Saw remained purposely behind to plan for the destruction of the AFPFL with the help of the white man who at the time had given 5 lakhs [500,000][1] to him [U Saw]. We have again come to know that while U Saw was in England some English capitalists aided him with lots of money. It will be interesting when the trial begins as all these secrets will be exposed.

No such "secrets" were exposed, however. But as confusion reigned, it was becoming obvious that U Saw was planning to take advantage of the situation. Within the first week of his incarceration, he had tried to make friends with the chief jailer, U San Tint. "If you help me, I'll make sure you get a big reward," U Saw had discreetly told San Tint. He did not know that he had approached the wrong person. San Tint was a Muslim—and also happened to be the nephew of Abdul Razak, who had been assassinated together with Aung San on 19 July.

San Tint immediately reported the matter to Tun Hla Oung, the CID chief. The next day, San Tint called on U Saw, who used even more cajolery to obtain a promise of help to escape in exchange for 50,000 Rupees. San Tint, under instructions, raised the bids: another 50,000 Rupees for Jail Superintendent Tin Maung and 100,000 Rupees for the Secretary of the Judicial Affairs Ministry, Justice Thaung Sein. It was then that attention was drawn to a mysterious connection involving some Britons.

On his next visit, the Chief Jailer demanded the money. This prompted U Saw to whisper that he had to contact one Captain David Vivian. Unbeknownst to U Saw, this British officer, an arms adviser to the Burma Police, was actually in another cell in Insein Jail. He had been arrested and charged with supplying U Saw with weapons the day after Aung San's assassination.

After 60 Bren guns had gone missing in June, the Assistant Commissioner of Police in Rangoon, Michael Busk, had actually suggested that additional security precautions be taken at the Secretariat, since that was where the cabinet always met. Any political rivalry at this volatile stage in Burma's modern history could easily erupt into a shoot-out. Aung San himself turned the suggestion down, saying that he felt secure in "the affections of his people".

Busk then asked for a warrant to search U Saw's house, which was turned down on political grounds. U Saw was a prime suspect—which was the reason his house was under constant surveillance. But it was only after the assassination on 19 July that U Saw's compound was searched at last, and some of the guns recovered. Subsequent investigations led to the Fytche Flats, which were raided in the afternoon of Sunday the 20th.

This David Vivian happened to be living there and at first he refused to let the police in. He demanded to see a search warrant. This was rejected by the police, led by ACP Busk and Assistant Superintendent U Thein Ohn, who burst into the flat—to more or less stumble on a stockpile of diamonds, gold, silver, and other jewelry. The first weapon to be found was a revolver hidden inside a suitcase that belonged to Vivian's wife. Half an hour later, a jeep-load of arms was discovered: three rifles, three revolvers, one Sten gun, hand grenades, more rifles, and a large quantity of ammunition. Some of the ammunition was carefully concealed in big boots which were found on the floor in the flat. Captain Vivian was taken into custody immediately .

The British captain's obvious involvement in gun-running was in itself not particularly astonishing; many officers of the armed forces in Burma made extra money on the side by selling weapons on the black market to anyone who was willing to buy them. Given the unsettled political situation in Burma, and the existence of several private pocket armies, there was certainly no shortage of customers. But U Saw seemed to know this young Captain Vivian well enough even to ask him for help to raise a substantial sum of money.

CID chief Tun Hla Oung became eager to investigate the matter when San Tint related the astonishing piece of information that U Saw wanted to contact this shadowy British captain. The Chief Jailer was encouraged to find out more and to act as the messenger. San Tint returned to U Saw, told him that he knew "where Captain Vivian lives"—and was handed a handwritten note, which he promised to deliver to the British officer. U Saw's first message to Captain Vivian was written in code:

Ghost limping every night. Green Bananas. Lemonade is the sweetheart of David.

San Tint handed the message over to Tun Hla Oung, who showed it to Justice Thaung Sein:

We considered it important enough to rush it to Prime Minister Thakin Nu at his home. He was as perplexed as we were, and so was the Home Minister, U Kyaw Nyein. We decided to encourage the correspondence.

The cryptic note was later delivered to Captain Vivian in his cell by San Tint, who pretended he was a "secret messenger from U Saw"—which was not entirely untrue. But the captain's reply to U Saw was even more puzzling: "I recognise the gentleman." U Saw then wrote in his next message: "I was the Sikh."
It was beginning to make sense for the investigators who read the cryptic notes. U Saw was apparently referring to a costume ball they had both attended, and he wanted to make absolutely sure that it was indeed Vivian he was communicating with. After this first exchange of letters, Vivian suddenly began referring to himself as "we" instead of "I". He also began mentioning what appeared to be an imposing figure: "We can arrange all that. Why don't you approach the tall gentleman?" Saw and Vivian's messages mentioned "a tall gentleman", and the police then sent a bogus reply from Vivian to Saw to contact the "tall gentleman" direct, upon which within the next few hours U Saw sent two messages—to one Mr. John Stewart Bingley of the British Council in Rangoon.

Shortly afterwards Tun Hla Oung in a clever stroke arrested two other British officers in connection with the theft some time previously of 200 Bren guns from the Botataung ordnance depot and 100,000 rounds of .303 ammunition from another army warehouse on Prome Road. This did not arouse any suspicion among the people he was trying to snare; the CID had been involved in investigating the theft since mid-July. One of the officers, Major J.A. Moore of the Indian Army Ordnance Corps, was actually Officer Commanding at the Base Ammunition Depot in Botataung. The other, Major C. Henry Young, served as Commander of the Indian Army Electrical and Mechanical Engineers (IAEME) Workshop Company in Rangoon.

On 15 July, four days before his assassination, Aung San himself had reported the disappearance of the weapons to the Governor, expressing his concern—especially about the great time-lag between loss and discovery. On 24 June, a party purporting to be police had arrived at the arms depot with what appeared to be duly signed, proper documents, and collected the weapons. The bogus police party had used an unmarked truck, not a proper police vehicle, which had caused some suspicion. But it was not until 14 July that the affair was brought to the attention of higher authorities. The weapons were still lost, and it was not clear in whose hands they were.

During their interrogation, Major Young readily admitted to his connections with U Saw: he actually lived in a house across Inya Lake from the *Galon* chief. U Saw had been in close contact with Young for some time and on one occasion had given a party at his Ady Road residence, which the British officer had attended. Captain Vivian had been there as well. It was at this party that Young had introduced U Saw to this Bingley of the British Council. During that encounter, Young claimed that Bingley had in a loud voice assured U Saw that "we're all prepared to help you fully".

My father showed the British major copies of U Saw's coded messages to Captain Vivian. Young, somewhat surprisingly, proceeded to unravel the mystery:

— "Ghost limping every night"—Young revealed that his own house was reputed to be haunted by a spectre with a limp.

— "Green bananas"—long green bananas of the Burmese *thee-hmwe* ("fragrant fruit") variety had been served at U Saw's party.

— "Lemonade is the sweetheart of David"—David was none other than the British major's own young son, who loved lemonade and was quaffing it at the party.

When the interrogation was over, Tun Hla Oung retreated to his office to ponder the astonishing revelation. The accusing finger now pointed at Bingley. He was also certainly bigger than most Burmese, but was he "the tall gentleman" Captain Vivian had referred to in one of his messages? There were many other tall men around as well, so Tun Hla Oung could not draw any definite conclusions at this stage.

Meanwhile, as the trial proceeded before the Special Tribunal in Insein, Ba Nyunt, the King's witness and Approver, made some remarkable confessions. On becoming a member of U Saw's *Myochit* Party, he had been assigned to three special duties: to collect arms, ammunition, and to raise funds. Ba Nyunt went on to reveal that it was he who on 24 June had procured 200 Bren guns from the Base Ordnance Depot at Botataung. The weapons were transported in one lot to U Saw's Ady Road residence in a three-ton lorry, which Ba Nyunt said he had driven. On the next mission, he collected exactly 100,000 rounds of .303 ammunition from another depot on Prome Road. The munitions that had been found in sealed containers in the lake behind U Saw's house on 20 July turned out to come from this consignment. It all seemed to fit.

Khin Maung Yin, another member of the gang, who also happened to be the nephew of U Saw's wife, stated in his eventual confession that he had made "contact . . . with one Major Young for the purchase of a sub-machine gun, three American carbines, one Sten gun, two Tommy guns, one Luger pistol, two revolvers and ammunition". Khin Maung Yin also spoke of "U Saw's contact with Major Moore and Captain Vivian and of the theft of Bren guns and ammunition from Ordnance Depots, and of their distribution in the district and their concealment in the waters by the side of the house."

Khin Maung Yin revealed too that Major Young "was in charge of a military transport camp situated on the land owned by him [U Saw] on Kokine Road".[2] He went on to mention one "Major Lance" from whom "U Saw . . . obtained a Springfield rifle, two Tommy guns and one carbine". This officer, whose full name was actually Major Peter Ernest Lancelot Daine, lived "in a two-storeyed bungalow by the side of the rubber factory at Kamayut".

U Saw was a frequent visitor to that bungalow. Major Daine served with the Intelligence Branch, Burma Command HQ, and was also Commander of the Base Ammunition Depot in Mingaladon just north of Rangoon.

The Tribunal was thus able to state that there was "strong reason to believe" that Majors Young and Daine had supplied U Saw with the firearms which had been used in the assassination of Aung San. Captain Vivian's role in the plot was to have forged the police document with which the weapons had been obtained from Botataung and the other arms depot. Vivian lived in Fytche Flats in Rangoon, which also housed other junior British officers plus some local businessmen, among them Malhotra—who appeared to have a very special relationship with these officers as well as with U Saw. Malhotra, who was of Indian origin, worked for Leele & Co, a British firm, and was especially close to Major Daine. This seemed to corroborate the theory that junior British officers in collusion with British financial interests were supporting U Saw, and possibly also inciting him to move against Aung San, whose leftist ideas annoyed certain circles within the Rangoon business community.

There were also other right-wing politicians who formed part of this anti-Aung San alliance. Dr. Ba Maw, the head of state of the Japanese puppet government during the occupation, was one of them. He was among the 800 possible suspects rounded up by Tun Hla Oung in the wake of the assassination. Another was veteran politician Thakin Ba Sein, who, together with Thakin Tun Oke, had led the "pro-Axis" faction of the Thirty Comrades, as opposed to the "Thakin Kodaw Hmaing" faction led by Aung San and Bo Let Ya. Tun Oke had led the last batch of eleven young nationalists to arrive in Japan, which included Thakin Shu Maung, alias Ne Win.

Together, they formed an extreme right-wing bloc that was closely connected with U Saw and foreign business. They were undoubtedly Aung San's rivals, and each one of these politicians aspired to lead the country from foreign domination to freedom, and then take the place of the British. But their interrogations did not reveal anything substantial that linked them to the assassination of Aung San. They were subsequently released.

The movements of the suspected British officers had been monitored for some time by plain-clothes police agents, dispatched by Tun Hla Oung and commanded by Captain Khan, U Saw's neighbour, whose car almost crashed into the vehicle of the assassins on 19 July. Khan's men, posing as fishermen, had spent hours on the shores of Inya Lake by a narrow inlet across from U Saw's residence, monitoring movements in and out of the compound even before the assassination took place. They had observed the coming and going of trucks and heavy equipment being unloaded. But, at that time, no one was exactly sure what kind of goods were being transported.

My father-in-law, Justice Thaung Sein, told me much later: "There is a saying in Burmese that only a diamond can cut another diamond, and Tun Hla Oung was a worthy opponent for the erstwhile *Galon Tat* commander." U Saw and his henchmen, whatever they had been planning to do, were obviously unaware of the formidable enemy they were up against.

The Governor, Sir Hubert Rance, cabled to London: "My own view is that the plan of certain elements of the opposition was to collect arms by stealth and gradually to prepare the way for armed strife and fight for power." Certainly, U Saw and his gang had enough weapons to start a civil war, probably with the support of Captain Vivian, Majors Young and Daine, and other, like-minded British officers. The testimony of gunman Khin Maung Yin during the trial had provided engrossing accounts of the furtive activities in U Saw's compound. Major Young's residence was four miles distant by road but only half an hour rowing time away. Khin Maung Yin testified that he and his comrades had made about seven or eight trips in rowing boats to transport guns across the lake. Cabin Island, half-way across, served as the shooting practice spot.

But whatever they had planned to do, it had been foiled in the aftermath of the assassination of Aung San. U Saw did not become the leader of the nation; he was a miserable prisoner who needed money urgently to pay his legal expenses and, hopefully, to buy his freedom as well. He sent a letter to a wealthy friend in Mandalay. Tun Hla Oung immediately had him arrested. U Saw sent similar pleas to other followers all over the country. They too were taken into custody.

Then, in a state of desperation, U Saw threw all caution to the winds and wrote an open letter to Bingley himself, briefly mentioning their rendezvous and "understanding"—and saying that he was now in dire financial straits and needed money. In the typical Burmese way, he added that he had "no wish to cause any inconvenience". But he did ask for a quick reply.

A police officer, posing as a newly released convict, was ordered to deliver the letter to Bingley personally at his house in Rangoon. Bingley took the envelope and opened it. Trusting the messenger perhaps too much, Bingley read the letter out loud in front of him. Blood drained from Bingley's face. He tore the letter to pieces and rushed inside with the shreds of paper in his hand. The undercover policeman could hear the toilet flush. Bingley then emerged through the door and screamed at him: "Get out of here! Get out immediately!"

Circumstantial evidence showed that Bingley and U Saw had a very special relationship. U Saw wrote two letters to Bingley, dated 22 and 23 August. Again, he asked for money and referred to one "VV"—presumably Captain Vivian. The letters talked not only of hopes of escape but also of threats to make disclosures which would have both internal and international repercussions. U Saw assured Bingley that the messenger bringing the letters could be trusted.

Bingley never received these letters. The police ordered the messenger to deliver one of them but, on arriving at Bingley's house, he was brushed aside by the angry Englishman. Bingley was packing his bags and moving out of his residence to spend a night at the Strand Hotel before catching the first available BOAC flying boat out of Burma. It was leaving the very next morning. Tun Hla Oung reported the matter to Home Minister Kyaw Nyein, who promptly called on Governor Sir Hubert Rance. Kyaw Nyein requested that Bingley be arrested immediately so he could be interrogated by the police. But Sir Hubert demurred, probably fearing that any hint of British complicity in the assassination of Burma's beloved leaders could result in violent reprisals against the European community in Burma. He asked the minister to spare the new suspect, at least for the moment.

Despite this, however, Tun Hla Oung was allowed to meet Bingley in his house before he moved out. The meeting lasted for five hours. The jittery Bingley revealed nothing. But it also appeared highly unlikely that Bingley had tried to respond to U Saw's letters, Tun Hla Oung concluded.

As Bingley, suitcases in hand, stepped on to the jetty at the embarkation point near the Strand some days later, Tun Hla Oung calmly walked up to him. He had a copy of U Saw's last undelivered letter to Bingley in his pocket. Bingley, already shocked by this unexpected confrontation with Tun Hla Oung, turned pale when the police commander showed him the letter: "Do you recognise this handwriting?"

Tun Hla Oung mentioned that he now had powers to arrest the Englishman if he so wanted. Bingley panicked: "I have diplomatic immunity! I can appeal to the Governor himself if you arrest me!" Tun Hla Oung retained his controlled composure: "The Governor has given U Nu's interim government the right to take whatever action it considers vital in this case."

By confronting Bingley in this way, it had been Tun Hla Oung's purpose to try and establish beyond doubt the link between the head of the British Council in Rangoon and the people who had carried out the assassination of Aung San and the other national leaders. In the end, however, Tun Hla Oung simply warned Bingley not to set foot in Burma again. Bingley quickly boarded his BOAC flying boat— and was never heard of again. Bingley left Burma on 4 September 1947, and his fate and subsequent whereabouts remain shrouded in mystery.

U Saw, of course, was completely unaware of what was happening outside. His world had shrunk to consist of only his cell in Insein Jail and the nearby court room. U Saw was languishing in captivity; any hope of escape was diminishing rapidly. But it could not have been only the fact that he was in jail that troubled him. He had been a detainee before; there had been his four-year sojourn in Uganda—throughout the entire Japanese occupation of Burma—and then again a short spell in jail for sedition when the war was over. He was even known to have bragged in his political campaigns that nine of his maternal uncles had been individually convicted of murder and that each of them had, on appeal to the High Court, been acquitted. But such bravado belonged to the past: this time U Saw could hope neither for a pardon nor for clemency.

U Saw began to write to Captain Vivian again, quite openly this time, an action which reflected desperation or despondency, or perhaps both. In one letter, U Saw asked Vivian what his place of refuge could be in the outside world. Vivian, rather intriguingly, wrote back suggesting Goa, a Portuguese enclave on the coast of India. Was it the planned haven for the conspirators? No one knows. Vivian, in any event, knew that part of the Indian subcontinent quite well. Although a professed Welshman, he had spent many of his early years in Bangalore.

Since no replies were forthcoming from Bingley—U Saw did not know that he had left the country—other contact persons had to be found outside the jail. U Saw composed yet another coded message:

Not a single fish in Inya Lake.

San Tint received the message with instructions to hand it over to an Indo-Burmese teashop owner in Dalla, a small town across the Rangoon river. The message was strange indeed. Inya Lake, close to U Saw's Ady Road residence, was teeming with fish and ubiquitous "No Fishing" signs were duly ignored, even by Captain Khan's men who had kept U Saw's residence under surveillance. What did the message mean?

An undercover police officer was assigned to deliver the note to this hitherto unknown accomplice of U Saw. He read it and pleaded apologetically that he could not possibly get U Saw the revolver he wanted! The teashop owner in Dalla was taken in for questioning. Finally, the message seemed to make sense. U Saw had hidden his illegally acquired weapons in sealed containers in the lake. "No fish" meant, of course, that there were no weapons left in the lake, as they had all been discovered by the authorities and confiscated. U Saw badly needed at least a simple handgun from another source.

Although the cryptic message had been deciphered, the interrogations of the teashop owner in Dalla, and others who were arrested at the same time, revealed little. Nevertheless, U Saw's network of contacts was shrinking rapidly.

Captain Vivian, too, was becoming resigned to his fate. One day, he approached Justice Thaung Sein saying that he wanted to "make a confession". U Thaung Sein advised Vivian that he could take his words down on paper, but such a document would not be strictly legal. Vivian nevertheless went on to tell the Justice how in April 1947 he had lost several of his comrades when a troop train was blown up near their base at Kalaw. The railway had been mined, and it was suspected that the sabotage had been carried out by members of the People's Volunteer Organisation, which, in effect, was Aung San's private militia force. The dead and wounded soldiers came from A Company of the 2nd battalion of the Welch Regiment, and Vivian, being a Welshman himself, felt very bitter about the incident. Consequently, he had allied himself with U Saw, Aung San's arch-rival.

Vivian's emotional account glossed over his previous admission to having received numerous favours from U Saw, including promises of future business concessions. Vivian was already a partner in a lorry transport concern together with Hteik Tin Maung Galay, one of U Saw's associates. This, more than any Welsh patriotic zeal, may have been the actual reason for Vivian's connections with U Saw.

Almost no hard evidence, however, could be unearthed from the interrogations of the British officers. Major Moore was never tried in court and Major Young received a two-year sentence—but was acquitted on appeal and left Burma immediately. Captain Vivian was sentenced to five years' imprisonment and two fines of 5,000 Rupees each. But in February 1949, when the Karen insurrection broke out and Insein was overrun by the rebels, he was set free along with all the other inmates of the notorious jail just north of Rangoon. Perhaps with no other place to go, Vivian joined the Karen rebels.

The military authorities in Rangoon still assume that Vivian was killed along with Karen rebel chief Saw Ba U Gyi at Kawkareik near the Thai border in August 1950. But he was not in Saw Ba U Gyi's camp that day; he stayed with the Karen insurgents for several years until he made it back to Britain via Thailand in the mid-1950s. Karen rebels who were close to the mysterious British captain during his time in the underground remember him as sullen, taciturn, and unwilling to talk about anything related to the assassination of Aung San. Following his return to Britain, Vivian lived in seclusion in Swansea, Wales, until he died in the late 1980s, taking whatever he knew about the assassination of Aung San with him to the grave.

So how deep ran the British involvement? Was it a conspiracy, planned in high places in London, to get rid of Aung San, as many Burmese at the time sincerely believed? Or were figures such as Vivian, Daine, Young, and Moore just private gun-runners and self-seeking adventurers? And exactly who was Bingley? Despite the professional nature of the arrest and trial of U Saw and his henchmen, the entire affair seemed to involve much more than met the eye.

5

Unanswered Questions

Although the actual trial of U Saw and his henchmen was to all appearances fair, even the respected Justice Thaung Sein was sceptical of some aspects of it. For instance, he noted that it was customary practice for the president of any tribunal to draft and read out a judgment—and although it was indeed read out by Justice Kyaw Myint on 30 December, the text had this time actually been submitted by U Aung Tha Gyaw, a member of the Special Tribunal that tried U Saw. And it just happened to be five days before Burma was to become independent, and any appeals to the Privy Council in London would be impossible. There had also been the initial difficulty in appointing members to the Special Tribunal. Many had already realised that the trial was bound to become a controversy that would haunt Burma for decades to come. Others were outright frightened: what if U Saw was not alone? How would his accomplices still at large—if there were any such people—react to the whole affair?

A few who tried to go further than the court's final judgment did not live to tell the tale. Colin Tooke, a former District Superintendent of Police in Hanthawaddy near Rangoon, secretly began investigating U Saw's case after the trial. He was convinced that there was something phoney about it. One night he returned home and his Burmese servant told him that his Alsatian dog "had got rabies". The dog therefore had to be shot and was now lying in a nearby river. Tooke could not believe this, as rabies takes time to develop, and his dog had been in perfect health that same morning. Tooke cut off the dog's head and took it to the veterinary surgeon in Rangoon, who confirmed that the dog had not contracted rabies. Tooke then found that his house had been burgled and all his files relating to the assassination of *Bogyokegyi* Aung San had gone. Some weeks later, Tooke died in hospital of "food poisoning".

Another person linked to the case to die under mysterious circumstances was U Tin Tut, the only bureaucrat that Aung San had trusted fully. Once a senior member of the ICS, Tin Tut served as Vice-Chancellor of Rangoon University in 1940. He accompanied U Saw to Britain and the US in 1942 and soon afterwards became Adviser for Reconstruction to the Burma Government, then in exile in Simla, India, from 1942 to 1945. After the war, he became Councillor for Finance and Revenue in the Governor's Council. He accompanied Aung San to London in January 1947 to negotiate Burma's independence—and it was during that trip that U Saw openly went against Aung San by refusing to sign the agreement with the British government.

Tin Tut was appointed Minister for Foreign Affairs in independent Burma's first government, but resigned in August 1948 to become Inspector General of the Auxiliary Forces with the rank of brigadier. He was also the founder and editor of the *New Times of Burma*, and happened to be the elder brother of Justice Kyaw Myint. It was widely believed at the time that Tin Tut was investigating U Saw's case for his newspaper.

One night in December 1948, as Tin Tut was leaving his office in the newspaper building, a hand grenade was thrown into his car. He died instantly, ironically within sight of the Secretariat, where Aung San had been killed a year-and-a-half before. "For the second time death removed a keystone of the Union", wrote Hugh Tinker in his classic study, *The Union of Burma*, adding that "Tin Tut was assassinated by the hirelings of a political opponent". But the identity of that "opponent" was never discovered.

Was Tin Tut's murder linked to his research into the assassination of Aung San? Or was it perhaps caused by rivalry within the armed forces? Shortly after Burma's independence in January 1948, the communists took up arms against the government, ethnic Karen rebels also rose up in arms, and several battalions of the then rather small and modest Burma Army mutinied. The most crucial of the units that remained loyal to the government was the 4th Burma Rifles, commanded by Brig.-Gen. Ne Win. Because of the mutinies, more organised units were raised in late 1948: the Union Auxiliary Forces, commanded by Tin Tut, and later also the Territorial Forces, *sitwundan*, which were responsible for local duties in the districts. Given his military as well as political clout, Tin Tut was a potential rival to many other officers in the Burma Army whose ambitions were not confined to military campaigns alone but who desired supreme political power.

Saw Yoo Shoo, an ethnic Karenni (Kayah) Lieutenant serving with the Union Military Police in Moulmein in 1947, still remembers how his British officer, Captain Michael Lilley, came to him on 18 July to say: "Aung San will shortly be assassinated. Be prepared to take over control of the town Moulmein if there is unrest." The next day, Aung San was assassinated. No one ever found out how much more Captain Lilley knew, because he also died suddenly in Moulmein shortly afterwards.

All these stories and other similar tales—unsubstantiated as well as substantiated—led many to believe that there was a great conspiracy against Aung San and his close associates, involving more people than U Saw. These people, real or imaginary, wanted to get rid of Aung San either out of sheer jealousy and lust for power, or because some quarters profoundly distrusted our young national hero. Aung San was Lord Mountbatten's favourite, but many junior British officers had not forgotten that he had sided with the Japanese during most of the war. Aung San's left-leaning political ideas were also disconcerting for the foreign business community in Rangoon, which sided with more conservative elements within the Burmese military. The involvement of Captain Vivian, and Majors Young and Daine, clearly indicated that this was the case.

However, the accusing finger of the Criminal Investigation Department of the Burma Police pointed firmly at U Saw, no one else. He not only had a motive but also had premeditated and masterminded the carnage in the Secretariat on 19 July. He did not physically pull the trigger, but then he was not accused of murder but of abetment. In contemporary Burmese-language publications about the event, there is no hint of conspiracy, nor references to distortion of the law in the trial proceedings.

The anniversary of the 19 July 1947 killings is still celebrated officially as a national holiday: *Arzani*, or Martyrs' Day. The Burmese then observe a day of mourning to honour their fallen leaders. The official media always publishes respectful editorials about the martyrs, linking their sacrifice to the endeavours of the present regime in which they try and list their biographies. In line with this tradition, the 19 July 1992 issue of the dreary, state-run organ of the ruling military, the *Working People's Daily*, ran a laudatory article, archaically headlined "Nurturing the Spirit of Patriotism and Nationalism":

> Today the State Law and Order Restoration Council is doing much to keep patriotism alive . . . patriotism has been given much prominence because of the hostile actions of various forces, sowing dissent, undermining national integrity and sovereignty with new variety of patterns, both on the political and economic front. (*sic*)

The article even went on to link the suppression of the 1988 uprising for democracy in Burma—during which the army gunned down thousands of peaceful young demonstrators—with the 1947 assassinations:

We have learnt lessons from having experienced the evils which occurred in the country. Anarchy and evils which we have experienced during the 1988 disturbances must be taken as lessons and their recurrence must be prevented.

While the martyrs are always given due honour, the norm is to say almost nothing about the assassins: who they were and why they killed Aung San. The above-mentioned article in the *Working People's Daily* for instance refers only in passing to the culprits, and then in very vague, ambiguous terms:

[19 July] was a dark day for the nation for the imperialists have struck through their henchmen. Although [Burma] regained independence a year later the seeds of discord sown by the imperialists sprouted into a problem that lingers on to this day. Multicoloured insurgent terrorists mushroomed throughout the country and have played havoc only to be put down by the *tatmadaw* [army].

The first exceptions to this rule came in September 1990 when the *Working People's Daily* ran a series of articles highlighting the British involvement in the assassination. This was probably an attempt to discredit the British government at a time when it was raising the issue of human-rights abuses in Burma in the United Nations in New York. Nevertheless, it fell far short of implicating anyone higher in the British hierarchy than Vivian and other junior officers in Rangoon who had links to shadowy businessmen such as Malhotra of Leele & Co.

The involvement of these people was common knowledge, and circumstantial evidence had already shown that these officers and businessmen, together with the mysterious J.S. Bingley of the British Council, secretly supported U Saw and his right-wing faction of politicians. The article would have had difficulty in accusing any higher-ranking officials, as the Governor's own cables to London at the time do not indicate knowledge of any greater British conspiracy other than the proven involvement of some elements of the free-wheeling Rangoon officer corps. Higher British authorities in Government House in Rangoon and in the Foreign Office in London were apparently as taken aback as anybody else when Aung San and his men were assassinated.[1]

The only proven "link" with London was U Saw's own brother, U Maung Maung Ji, who had raised some funds for his defence. He had also written some letters to the editor of *The Times*, questioning whether U Saw should have been deprived of the right to appeal to the Privy Council in England. He would have been entitled to this right had it not been for the constitutional changes which took place before the rather hastened termination of the case.

But even some people in Britain suspected that certain circles in London had supported the plot to get rid of Aung San. With him gone and U Saw installed as the new Prime Minister, Burma might have been kept in the British fold. In the House of Commons on 21 July 1947—two days after the assassination—Tom Driberg, a Labour MP, expressed "the real, deep sorrow that members feel on this side of the House" who had learned to respect Aung San and his colleagues, but alleged that "the moral guilt of the assassinations attaches less perhaps to the brutal elements in Rangoon than to the comfortable Conservative gentlemen here who incited to treachery and sabotage". Driberg was jeered by his opponents, and the Labour Government as well as the Conservative opposition joined in expressing deep regret and disclaiming any complicity in the crime.

A much more intriguing series of articles appeared in the *Working People's Daily* in the period 17–22 November 1990. They referred rather oddly to "Senior General Saw Maung's speech in a Textile Mill in Meiktila on 13 November", and were clearly aimed at exaggerating the role of Ne Win in the independence struggle at the expense of that of Aung San. The newspaper also reproduced some old telegrams from the colonial authorities in Rangoon to London, in which Ne Win was mentioned in favourable terms:

> [I] had anticipated Aung San's recommendation [for the post as Defence Minister] would lie between Hla Pe [Bo Let Ya] and Ne Win. Latter based on good opinions from 4 Corps with whom he has been working as PBF [Patriotic Burmese Forces; ex-BIA] comd and seemed the more promising candidate from military point of view. [However] Hla Pe may well be the more popular choice.

Another document, published in facsimile in the *Working People's Daily*, quoted British Chief of Staff General Templer as saying that "the perpetual suspicions of the Burmese were extremely tiresome [but] we were very willing to do all we reasonably could to help General Ne Win".

Who Killed Aung San?

Until then, Aung San's name had been sacrosanct in Burma: the deeply revered *bogyokegyi* was the father of the nation as well as the father of the army. Ne Win's main claim to supreme leadership for many years was that he had been a member of the Thirty Comrades and hence a brother-in-arms of Aung San. The fact that Aung San and Ne Win belonged to opposite factions of the Thirty Comrades, and that the two were never on especially friendly terms with one another, was always conveniently forgotten by the official media.

However, in 1988, Ne Win's claim to have inherited the Aung San legacy was openly challenged by Aung San Suu Kyi, the *bogyoke's* daughter, who emerged as the main leader of the pro-democracy movement that swept Burma in that year. Ne Win had her placed under house arrest on 20 July 1989—the day after *Arzani* Day.[2] Aung San Suu Kyi had planned to lead a massive march through Rangoon to the Martyrs' Mausoleum to honour her fallen father and his comrades, and Ne Win's army had responded by threatening to shoot any people who showed up for the event. The march was cancelled and scores of people were arrested.

The November 1990 series in the state-run media came more than a year after that, probably in an attempt to shake off the Aung San legacy and substitute it with reverence for Ne Win, whose supreme authority was then being challenged by the immensely popular Aung San Suu Kyi. But there was more to come. From 28 June to 2 July 1991, the *Working People's Daily* reproduced in facsimile a whole series of articles from U Saw's old newspaper, the *Sun*, attacking Aung San. Even hilarious cartoons ridiculing Aung San were reproduced, along with U Saw's verbal assaults on our national hero.

Although the commentary made it sound as if the articles were being reprinted to show "one-sided personal, policy and organisational attacks . . . dripping with scorn and jibes" (*sic*), the timing of the reappearance of these old articles did not escape the attention of Burmese readers. Aung San Suu Kyi had spent more than two years under house arrest and she had just been nominated by Czechoslovak President Vaclav Havel for the 1991 Nobel Peace Prize. Almost simultaneously, the state-run newspaper also ran a series about the history of "the leadership of the *tatmadaw*", again stressing Ne Win's crucial role in building up Burma's armed forces.

These series of articles in the *Working People's Daily* of course raise the crucial question around which most conspiracy theories have centred: did Ne Win scheme to get rid of Aung San in order to become the supreme leader himself? Was U Saw framed and only a pawn in a much more sinister plot? That Ne Win perceived Aung San as a rival—and the only person standing between himself and supreme power—was obvious. Their quarrels during their time in Tokyo as members of the

Thirty Comrades were also well known and documented by other members of the young team in Japan.

In short, three opinions prevail: the trial was fair and U Saw was the main culprit; U Saw was framed and the entire trial a travesty of justice; and U Saw was both guilty and framed. The first opinion is what most Burmese themselves believe, and it is also the official version as documented by the Burmese police authorities as well as Burmese writers. The second theory has adherents among many British officials who served in Burma in the late 1940s and now live in Britain. The third school of thought has only recently surfaced, primarily among some dissident Burmese exiles.

The only known published account to support the second opinion appeared in a bulletin published by the Karen National Union (KNU) in April 1986, almost four decades after the ghastly assassination. An article entitled "Who really killed Aung San?" and written by "Our Rangoon Correspondent" was featured in it. The introduction began with these two paragraphs:

> The mysterious assassination of Burma's Prime Minister Aung San in July 1947 was one of the major turning points in the Karen struggle for liberation. Although 39 years have passed, the real plotters of the murder have never been identified in public. The facts in the case have never been settled.
>
> Strong evidence exists that the trial and conviction of U Saw was a frame-up, designed to turn attention from the real conspirators. If U Saw was framed, who really murdered Burma's independence leaders? Is there any truth to persisting rumours that General Ne Win, Prime Minister U Nu and others may have been involved?

The article goes on to propound that Aung San had planned to "make major concessions to the Karens and other minorities...against the will of U Nu, Ne Win and other hard-line Burmans", including Home Minister Kyaw Nyein and another Socialist stalwart, Bo Khin Maung Gale. The most astonishing claim, however, was that one Saw Sein Hmon, the ethnic Karen District Superintendent of Police of Insein—a township north of Rangoon with a large Karen population—was ordered to arrest U Saw on the morning of 19 July, "which he promptly did at 9 a.m.", well before the actual assassination. "At the time U Saw was doing nothing unusual, only spending the morning with members of his family", Saw Sein Hmon said—according to the article. Saw Sein Hmon was then supposedly transferred to Pegu overnight to become DSP there.

The claim that U Saw was arrested by Saw Sein Hmon on the morning of 19 July—instead of in the afternoon by my father, Tun Hla Oung—is outright preposterous. Captain Khan, who testified during the trial that he had seen U Saw receive the assassins at 11 a.m. as they were returning from the Secretariat, could also not have been wrong about the time of the arrest. He was U Saw's neighbour and had kept him and his house under surveillance for quite some time. Neither U Saw, nor anyone else apart from the author of the article in the KNU Bulletin, has ever mentioned the supposed early morning arrest. Ba Nyunt, the Approver, also confirmed that the police surrounded U Saw's residence at 2 p.m.

However, to look into other, more credible claims made by the article, it is worth noting the allegation of involvement by "hard-line Burmans" such as U Nu (formerly Thakin Nu) and General Ne Win. Bloody clashes had indeed occurred between allegedly "pro-British" Karen communities (many Karens had sided with the Allies during the war) and unruly elements of the Burma Independence Army following the British retreat from Burma. These communal frictions escalated into civil war after Burma's independence, when the KNU went underground.

But even so, U Nu was probably one of the most sympathetic of the Burman leaders towards the Karens. In September 1948, before the Karen insurrection broke out, he had even appointed a Regional Autonomy Commission to look into Karen demands. Soon thereafter, in February 1949, when war was raging between the Karens and government forces, U Nu still advocated a peaceful solution, demeaning him with the nickname "Karen Nu" among Burman hard-liners who wanted to crush the rebellion with military might alone.

Any animosity that the KNU felt against U Nu probably arose long after these events. He was arrested when General Ne Win staged his *coup d'état* and seized power in March 1962 and was not released until October 1966. The wily dictator then set up an advisory body comprising 21 former state leaders, including U Nu, to assist in returning Burma to a more constitutional system of government. The majority of the 21 recommended a return to the multi-party democracy and free-market economy of pre-1962 days instead of the one-party dictatorship under the Burma Socialist Programme Party which Ne Win had introduced in 1962.

Ne Win rejected the suggestion on 2 June 1969, and U Nu left the country in disappointment. He journeyed to London where on 29 August he announced his plans to organise armed resistance against Ne Win's military regime. Eventually, this "war of liberation" began from sanctuaries along the Thai border. The armed wing of U Nu's movement, called the Patriotic Liberation Army (PLA), was led by some well-known Burma Army veterans: Bo Let Ya, Bo Yan Naing, and

Bohmu Aung of the Thirty Comrades; Brig. Henson Kya Doe, an ethnic Karen who had been Chief of Operations in the Burma Army immediately after independence; and Air Commodore Tommy Clift, former chief of the Burma Air Force.

U Nu's movement signed an agreement with the KNU and ethnic Mon rebels, also based along the Thai-Burma border, for joint operations, but disputes soon occurred over the right of secession which had been provided for the Shan and Kayah states under Burma's first, 1947 Constitution. Now other ethnic minorities, including the Karens and the Mons, wanted assurances from U Nu that they too would be given this right once the military regime had been overthrown.

U Nu, who favoured constitutional safeguards for ethnic rights as against secessional concessions, left Thailand sadly disillusioned in July 1973, after handing over his leadership position to Bo Let Ya. A patriot of the highest calibre and a close personal friend of Aung San, Bo Let Ya was killed in November 1978 when the KNU attacked his camp in what appeared to be a misunderstanding between the two armed groups. The PLA subsequently fell into disarray and no armed Burman opposition was to exist until exactly ten years later, when thousands of pro-democracy students fled the massacres in Rangoon and elsewhere to take refuge in the same border areas and from there make renewed attempts to fight the military government in Rangoon.

General Ne Win, the other Burman leader accused in the KNU Bulletin, however, is a person fundamentally different from U Nu. It is worth noting that the first detailed telegram from the Governor's office in Rangoon to London about Aung San's assassination actually stated that the gunmen had been identified as members of Ne Win's 4th Burma Rifles.[3] This piece of puzzling information was later dropped from official cables. Was it a mistake or did the authorities for political reasons refrain from further investigating the initial report? We shall never know, but the wily commander of the 4th Burma Rifles has haunted the Burmese scene ever since.

A Sino-Burman, born Shu Maung in 1911, Ne Win is four years junior to U Nu and five senior in age to Aung San. Although he was a member of the Thirty Comrades, it was not until 1946 that Ne Win began his ruthless and determined climb to the top. After independence, when the Communists and the PVO went underground and the 1st and 3rd Burma Rifles mutinied, Ne Win's 4th Burma Rifles became a main pillar of support for the government in Rangoon. But in order to diversify the defence of the state, new units such as Tin Tut's Union Auxiliary Forces were raised.

To forge national unity, the government even appointed an ethnic Karen, Lieut.-Gen. Smith-Dun, Commander in Chief of the army. Under him were two deputy commanders: Ne Win, now Major-General, and my father, Maj.-Gen. Tun Hla Oung, Inspector General of Police. Tin Tut, number four in the military hierarchy, was killed in late 1948 by an unidentified assassin. And a few months later, Smith-Dun was asked to take "indefinite leave" because of the outbreak of the Karen rebellion, although he had remained loyal to the government. Smith-Dun was relieved and placed on the inactive list, and went into self-imposed exile in the Kachin State.

Tun Hla Oung was the first Burman to obtain entrance to the Royal Military College at Sandhurst, and was awarded he King's Commission on graduation in 1922. He was sent to London in late 1948 to become Military Attaché at the Burmese Embassy there, a position much inferior to the one he had previously held. On completing his tenure in Britain in 1951, he left for home. But when his ship reached the port of Colombo in Ceylon (now Sri Lanka), he was met by Burmese intelligence officers. Inexplicably, Tun Hla Oung's passport was revoked and he was left stranded in Ceylon until 1954. Of Burma's original top four military officers in Burma, by 1949 only Ne Win remained.

Ne Win was—and still is—without doubt a Machiavellian power-monger, and most Burmese see his hand in the removal of political and military rivals in the late 1940s and, to an even greater extent, thereafter. It is also plausible to assume that he must have perceived Aung San's removal from the scene in 1947 with glee, as his main contender for supreme power had been done away with. But was he capable of masterminding a plot, to instigate U Saw to kill Aung San and his colleagues? It may seem far-fetched, but this is exactly what some Burmese exiles today believe.

This "third opinion" has most recently been expressed in a booklet which was published in Fort Lauderdale, USA, in May 1992. The booklet was written by Dr. Kyin Ho, alias Naing Win, a Burmese doctor who now works in Florida. It is based on conversations with a younger brother of Bo Let Ya, Mya Hlaing, an erstwhile War Office clerk who went to the US for medical treatment in July 1987. Dr. Kyin Ho treated Mya Hlaing free of charge as an old friend. In return, Mya Hlaing began to reveal what he knew about Aung San's assassination. Mya Hlaing made the astonishing revelation that he and another prominent Burmese at that time, Rangoon Ba Swe, were trained for two months to make a fake attempt on U Saw's life—and blame it on Aung San. The organisers of this plot were Ne Win and his close associate, Brig.-Gen. Aung Gyi, Mya Hlaing claimed.

According to Mya Hlaing's story, as retold by Dr. Kyin Ho:

One day, as I was about to go home after work at the War Office my *saya* [teacher], Bo Aung Gyi, told me: "You, Ko Mya Hlaing, don't go home. Come to my house. There is an important matter we have to discuss." I went along. He then asked: "How much money have you got?" I replied that I had about one or two lakhs or so [100,000–200,000 Kyats], and he remarked: "OK, that should be adequate for your household. We have a certain duty to perform. Stay at my home. You can return when all the work is done." I ended up staying [with Bo Aung Gyi] for two months. Rangoon Ba Swe, however, stayed in Bo Ne Win's house, where he practiced shooting with a gun.

To be absolutely sure, we had to train some more [despite the fact that Rangoon Ba Swe was a crack shot]. We then had to study in minute detail the movements of U Saw: when he left his house to go to his office and when he returned . . . on the day of the attempt on U Saw's life, he came in his big black car, sitting by the side of his driver. We followed them from behind. When we reached a good spot, I [the driver of our vehicle] overtook his car. It was then that Rangoon Ba Swe pulled the trigger. The first shot grazed U Saw's forehead. That was the most important shot. Rangoon Ba Swe then fired a second shot. It did not hit U Saw, as he had slid off his seat. A third shot was fired into the air.

Rangoon Ba Swe then shouted: "Heh! Mya Hlaing! Drive away!" I must have done so very fast because I cannot even recollect how we reached home. The gun that was used belonged to Ne Win personally . . . U Saw never knew that Rangoon Ba Swe and I had carried out the plot . . . this was a matter that only four of us—Bo Ne Win, Bo Aung Gyi, Rangoon Ba Swe and myself—knew about.

Dr. Kyin Ho adds that Ne Win was jealous of Aung San and always lived in fear of him. At this time, also, Aung San was scolding the profligate Ne Win. Bo Ne Win, with the mind of a race-goer,[4] plotted that an attempt would be made on U Saw without taking his life. U Saw would then retaliate by taking revenge on Aung San—the two gunmen in the car that day wore the uniforms of Aung San's "private army", the PVO—by being convinced that he was behind the assassination attempt.

All the details of this story—except the identities of the gunmen and their motives—were already recorded in the late 1940s. The attempt on U Saw's life on 21 September 1946, ten months before Aung San was killed, and the purported PVO involvement in the incident, had indeed been quoted as a motive for the assassination even during the trial. But how reliable was Mya Hlaing's account? No one will ever find out. Rangoon Ba Swe died of brain cancer quite some time ago, while Mya Hlaing passed away in a Rangoon hospital in 1991, a few years after his visit to Florida.

So who really killed Aung San? The question mark must be a large one, since nothing short of a death-bed confession from any possible mastermind of a greater plot could effectively establish the truth. Since the conclusion of the trial, which found U Saw—and nobody else—guilty, nothing really substantial has been unearthed about the possible involvement of more accomplices. Mya Hlaing's "confession" is intriguing and has a certain ring of truth to it. But can history be revised on the basis of something he allegedly said in a private conversation to which there were no independent witnesses? The whole truth may never be known, as indeed is the case with the assassination of US President John F. Kennedy and many other unsolved mysteries in world history. But based on circumstantial evidence and numerous loose ends, it is reasonable to assume that U Saw was not alone.

Whatever the case, and perhaps much more importantly in a broader historical context, the assassination of Aung San has left a legacy of violence and distrust that still lingers today, 45 years—or almost two generations—after U Saw's gunmen stormed into the Secretariat in downtown Rangoon and in cold blood gunned down Burma's best-respected political leaders.

6

A Legacy of Violence

As if emulating the proud peacock from Burma's national emblem, he strutted about, shaking hands with people around him and bidding them farewell. Slowly and calmly, but with a trace of a smile, U Saw walked the pathway up to the gallows. It was dawn, 8 May 1948. Burma had been independent for four months and four days, and more than ten months had passed since the assassination of Aung San and his colleagues. In a final gesture of bravado, in keeping with his motto—"He who dares to kill should dare to die"—U Saw firmly refused the hood to mask his sight.

With a brash bold look, he inspected the few who had gathered to witness his rendezvous with destiny. The executioner put the noose around his neck and pulled on the rope. Within seconds, the villain was dead. Maung Soe, Thet Hnin and Hmon Gyi followed their leader to the gallows at Insein Jail. Maung Sein and Yan Gyi Aung were executed in Rangoon.

The task of the Tribunal was done. The Law had triumphed over individual adventurism—but U Saw and his men left behind a legacy of violence in Burmese politics from which the nation has suffered to this day. Dr. Ba Maw, the war-time leader of the Burmese nationalists, had remarked even before Aung San's assassination:

Worship of the gun has become a fetish. The Burmese learned two things from the Japanese: the technique of leadership based on mass organisation; and the glamour and power of armed men. It is not elections that are going to decide the future of Burma, but the gun. All you want in Burmese politics is to start on the winning side and to have plenty of guns.

Dr. Ba Maw's cynical prophecy became reality with U Saw. *Thoke-thin-ye*—to remove rivals by complete elimination in order to wrest the crown and ascend the throne—is the game Burmese power-mongers play even today. The first to realise this was actually Aung San himself. In early 1946, he met the then British Governor, Sir Reginald Dorman-Smith, and confided in him about his loneliness and difficulty in making friends. Then, with tears in his eyes, Aung San said: "How long do national heroes last? Not long in this country; they have too many enemies. Three years is the most they can hope to survive. I do not give myself more than another eighteen months of life."

About eighteen months later and just six days before he lost his life, Aung San addressed a public meeting in Rangoon. It was 13 July and he spoke on the progress of the newly elected Constituent Assembly. To people who attended the meeting, it sounded like a farewell speech, and Aung San ominously concluded by beginning his last sentence with: "Let me leave word with you . . ."

The elimination of almost the entire cabinet in July 1947 was the first and most savage outcome of the concept of *thoke-thin-ye*. The next institution to face the same fate was the army. Historical circumstances in an emergency had placed Ne Win, the former *thakin* turned soldier in a partnership with the three British-trained, highly educated officers: Brig. Tin Tut, Maj.-Gen. Tun Hla Oung and Lieut-Gen. Smith-Dun. Ne Win must have felt acutely uncomfortable with the situation, and it was not long before these rivals were either killed or removed from power.

My father, Tun Hla Oung, and Smith-Dun were not the only ones to be purged without any valid reason. Smith-Dun had most probably been selected in order to appease his fellow Karens and other frontier peoples; and for the same reason two more Karens had also been selected for top positions in the armed forces: Brig. Kya Doe, a Sandhurst graduate, became chief of operations and Wing Commander Shi Sho chief of the air force. They were dismissed from service along with Smith-Dun. Yet, these three top Karens in the armed forces were unquestionably among those who had remained loyal to the government when the KNU resorted to armed struggle in January 1949. Thus, their dismissal was either based on purely racial grounds, or caused by a rival who had found a convenient excuse to get rid of them.

Part of Ne Win's obsession with eliminating every potential rival most likely stems from feelings of inferiority. As a youth, Shu Maung—as Ne Win was known at that time—had dropped out from Judson College and obtained a junior clerical job at the Churchill Road (Komin Kochin) branch post office in suburban Rangoon. His official biographer, Dr. Maung Maung, claims in his *Burma and General Ne Win* that this enabled the young *thakin* to "discreetly check the mail and the telegrams to discover what the police were up to and then warn his comrades. His intelligence was keen. The job also provided a good listening post."

None of his old comrades from those days can recall being warned by Ne Win about anything. Dr. Maung Maung's imaginative account of Ne Win's young days goes on to claim that his frequent visits to the race course in Rangoon were another cover for his political activities: "The Turf Club was the gathering ground of so many people, and his ears were pricked not for racing tips only. He would also go around and ask his friends, who were working in different government offices, for the latest news."

Perhaps predictably, apologists like Dr. Maung Maung were the only ones to survive Ne Win's frequent purges. Dr. Maung Maung was weak, he did not pose any threat to Ne Win, and he was willing to sacrifice his academic credentials to become a sycophant. For a brief period in August–September 1988, the nondescript Dr. Maung Maung was even made President of the Union and Chairman of the only legally permitted political organisation in Burma at that time, the Burma Socialist Programme Party (BSPP).

But other, more competent people became victims of the *thoke-thin-ye* policy. Bo Let Ya, one of the closest associates of Aung San in his student days, slipped into oblivion after independence, although *bogyokegyi* had recommended him for the post of head of the new Burma Army. Another of Aung San's closest friends, Bo Kyaw Zaw, remained in the army until the mid-1950s and conducted several successful campaigns against renegade Kuomintang forces from Yunnan which had intruded into Burma following the communist victory in China.

Kyaw Zaw was the most popular commander in the early 1950s; he was also the only one of the Thirty Comrades who remained on active duty in the Burma Army apart from Ne Win himself. The deeply revered Thirty Comrades occupy an almost mythical position in modern Burmese history; they were the fathers of Burma's independence and the founders of the country's armed forces. Ne Win therefore did not have to worry too much about junior BIA, BDA, and BNA officers. Kyaw Zaw was his only contender for power over the army.

Bertil Lintner writes in *Outrage*:

But then, in 1956, a mopping-up operation codenamed *Aung Marga* ('Victory Path') was mounted against the CPB in upper Burma and some secret documents were found in a captured communist camp. Without producing any evidence or direct connection, Kyaw Zaw was accused of being guilty of the leak. The public was shocked and many did not know what to believe. However, Kyaw Zaw was dismissed from the army and briefly held in detention. In 1957, Kyaw Zaw was released since no evidence had yet surfaced to substantiate the allegations against him. But his career was ruined and he settled down in Sanchaung in Rangoon with a modest pension from the army."

The army was gaining in strength, partly because of the insurgencies, and Ne Win was busy strengthening his grip on the *tatmadaw*. In a surprise move in October 1958, he was nominated by the parliament to serve as Prime Minister. The ruling Anti-Fascist People's Freedom League had split into two factions, a "Clean" AFPFL led by U Nu and a "Stable" AFPFL under Kyaw Nyein and Ba Swe, the two socialist leaders, and as a result a major political crisis had emerged. Ne Win's mandate was to head a caretaker government awaiting new elections.

The achievements of Ne Win's caretaker administration were actually laudable. Rangoon was cleaned up, law and order was restored, and large numbers of insurgents surrendered on terms which were fair to both sides. This success, however, was almost entirely due to qualified and efficient civilians within the administration, and a few senior army officers, mostly veterans from the Second World War. The policy was capitalistic and pragmatic, and it worked. In 1960, the promised elections were also held and Ne Win favoured the faction led by Kyaw Nyein and Ba Swe. But U Nu returned to power with a landslide victory, underscoring the popularity he still enjoyed despite the crisis of 1958. The electorate had also demonstrated their distrust of the army's meddling in politics by rejecting the Ba Swe-Kyaw Nyein faction.

But disaster struck the nation on 2 March 1962. The popularly elected Prime Minister, all ministers, heads of the ethnic minority states of the Union, and everyone else who could possibly pose any opposition, were arrested. The democratic constitution of 1947 was scrapped; Burma's federal structure gave way to a highly centralised state machinery ruled by the military. The reason given for the coup was "the greatly deteriorating conditions of the Union". Others who remember these days in Rangoon, like myself, saw no such signs. The insurgencies had been largely contained, the economy was doing well and the political climate had stabilised considerably after the 1960 election.

Ne Win's *coup d'état* has often been described as bloodless, but this was not the case. Its first victim was Sai Myee, the 17-year-old son of Sao Shwe Thaike, who in 1948-52 had served as Burma's first president. He was one of the main leaders of the Shans and a firm advocate of maintaining Burma's unity through federalism. My own home in those days was only a few hundred yards from Sao Shwe Thaike's Rangoon residence at the junction of Kokine and Goodliffe Roads.

I had visited him on several occasions, and more frequently his eldest daughter and her husband, who lived in an apartment annexed to the actual residence. Chao Tzang Yawnghwe (Eugene Thaike) and Hso Harn Pha, Sai Myee's elder brothers now live in Canada, and Harn has given me following account of what happened during the night of the coup:

Between one and two o'clock that morning, the army surrounded our 9-acre compound at 74 Kokine Road, Rangoon. They took into custody all the servants, employees, retainers, and guards, and their families, who lived on the grounds. The soldiers then advanced on the house.

From a distance of less than 100 feet, they indiscriminately opened fire with automatic weapons from all directions. The confused gunfire continued for about 45 minutes. No one knew why they started firing and why they stopped.

At the first sound of gunfire, Eugene (23 years), one of my older brothers, rolled off his bed and crawled out of his bedroom. He found the front door wide open.

Eugene's bed was directly in front of an open window on the ground floor. Had he sat up instead of rolling off the bed, he would not have been alive today. His white mosquito net was riddled with bullet holes.

On finding that Myee (17 years), another one of my older brothers, was missing, my father went downstairs and found Eugene by the open front door. They shut the front door and locked and bolted it.

In the morning, it was found that the front door was riddled with bullet holes. How either my father or Eugene escaped being shot is a mystery.

Everyone who saw the damage to the building afterwards, agrees that all my family could have been killed by the gunfire. What saved us was the fact that the building was a pre-war colonial-style house. The brick wall on the ground floor was about 18 inches thick and only the upper floor was made of wood.

Most of the bullets fired did not penetrate the thick walls. Given the short distance the troops were firing from the thickness of the walls on the ground floor were at a very steep angle and did little harm.

After they stopped shooting soldiers brought one of the people who lived in our compound to the front door to explain that there had been a coup. They ordered the door opened. My father then opened the front door and was arrested.

My father and Eugene were taken through the fields to a hole that the soldiers had made in the hedge that surrounded our property. My father was then taken away in a car. Eugene was escorted back to the house and the rest of us were told to come out.

On the way back to the house, one of the officers told Eugene that they had shot somebody—maybe his brother.

The soldiers then started a search of the house. Unfortunately for them, one of their bullets had hit the fuse box and the house was in total darkness. Fearing an ambush, they made Eugene enter each room ahead of them.

They found nothing except for two automatic pistols that had been presented to my father by the Czechoslovakian government on his resent official visit. They had both been locked for safety in my father's cupboard.

Before withdrawing from the scene later in the morning, an officer ordered the men to pick up their spent cartridges. However, we found about a hundred cartridge shells which were overlooked by the soldiers under some trees and bushes.

As the day broke, the soldiers left and a search began for Myee. His body was found in a flower bed to the left of the front porch. He had been shot in he head and foot. A ceremonial spear was found near his body.

On the night of March 1, Myee had complained of some stomach trouble. We can only assume that he was not sleeping soundly, heard some sounds in the still night and went out to investigate.

The nervous soldiers may have panicked, shot him and sent off a chain reaction, or he might have been hit as the troops opened fire according to a pre-determined plan.

In the morning the police came to investigate. They had been prevented from coming earlier by soldiers who had taken over the police station. A murder case was filed.

The press also arrived and were fully informed of events. However, when they got back to their offices, they were prevented from reporting the true story. Instead, the Revolutionary Council issued a statement that said troops carrying out their duty had met with resistance and had been forced in self defence, to open fire accidentally killing Sao Shwe Thaike's son.

Chao Tzang had also given an intense account of his traumatic experiences on that night of iniquity in his book "*The Shan of Burma—Memoirs of a Shan Exile*."

I was rudely awakened at about 4 a.m. on the morning of 2 March 1962, by sounds of gunfire, faintly at first but growing louder as I grew more awake. The gunfire was directly outside the home, and bullets smashed through window panes and frames, thudded against or ricochetted off the walls. A military unit had crept up to our home in the dark, and surrounded it on two sides, had opened fire. My younger brother Chao Mee who was only seventeen years old was killed 'while resisting the armed forces in its performance of duty', according to the authorities concerned.

Chao Tzang stressed these observations in the "Notes" annexed to this chapter.

[28] "Strangely enough not a shot was fired at the residence of the Prime Minister and cabinet ministers which were heavily guarded by paramilitary police."

The authoritarian rule went relentlessly on with their military killing machine grinding innocent people in its path. A once loved and proud *tatmadaw* had been turned into a private army of the dictator to wage a genocidal war to keep him in power. Chao Tzang then inconsolably recalled his young brother's murder with these words: "When I examined my brother, I found two wounds. A rifle bullet had ripped into his ankle and there was another hole, from a small calibre round, in the back of his head. It was evidently a cold-blooded killing. He was, it can be said, the first of the many thousands of unarmed young citizens of Burma killed with calculated coldness by the military regime."

The ex-President himself was led away in captivity that morning and "expired" in jail in October. No details were ever made public. In Shan State itself, the popular *sawbwa* of Hsipaw, Sao Kya Hseng, was also taken away by the military, never to return to his family. He is believed to have been extrajudicially executed at Ba Htoo Myo army camp, north of Taunggyi, shortly after Ne Win's takeover.

In the capital, student unrest broke out in July, when it became clear that the military this time was not in for a brief "caretaker" period, as in 1958–60, but that they had seized power with the intention of holding on to it. Rabid ideologues such as Ba Nyein and Thein Pe Myint (Thakin Thein Pe) had been called in to support Ne Win's new policies, the so-called Burmese Way to Socialism. A return to democracy seemed remote, and the students naturally protested. Their demonstrations were met with violence and brutality.

On 7 July, four months after the actual takeover, troops surrounded the Rangoon University campus and opened fire with automatic weapons and machineguns. The official death toll was a ludicrously low 15; eye-witnesses say the victims were in the hundreds. The following day, the army even dynamited the historic Students' Union Building, the cradle of modern Burmese nationalism, where Aung San, Kyaw Nyein, U Nu, Ba Swe, and many other young *thakins* who later became state leaders had first met in the 1930s.

Ne Win tolerated no opposition. He had already arrested Kyaw Nyein and Ba Swe, whom he had favoured during the 1960 election. Also his erstwhile mentors, Thakins Tun Oke and Ba Sein, had all but vanished from public life; they were senior to Ne Win and were therefore shunted aside.

Even within the ruling junta, purges began after a year or so, as the military put its Burmese Way to Socialism into practice. The previously free press was strangled and private businesses were nationalised, that is, taken over by the army. All political parties—except Ne Win's own BSPP—were banned. But not everyone agreed to this: in 1963, Ne Win's heir apparent and long-time associate, Brig.-Gen. Aung Gyi, was sacked from the Revolutionary Council and imprisoned. Total submission was required to survive in the new Burma that the military was creating: a Burma built not on trust and consensus, but under dictatorial rule by one man alone.

Student unrest shook Burma again in the mid-1970s. U Thant, the former Secretary-General of the UN and one of Burma's internationally best-known personalities, had died in New York on 25 November 1974. His body was flown back to Rangoon for burial. Ne Win, acutely jealous of the popular and well-respected U Thant, wanted to bury him in an obscure cemetery on the outskirts of Rangoon. The students, however, wanted a state funeral for the national hero. They seized the coffin and carried it away to the campus of Rangoon University. Buddhist monks joined in the movement—which, perhaps predictably, was crushed in cold blood. Troops opened fire on the students and, again, hundreds of unarmed youths were mowed down mercilessly. The official casualty toll was nine killed, 74 wounded, and 1,800 arrested.

The next big purge of the army came two years after the U Thant incident, when some young officers, graduates from the Defence Services Academy in Maymyo, tried to get rid of Ne Win. Led by a young army Captain, Ohn Kyaw Myint, they had a dream of a freer, more democratic Burma. However, the plot was discovered and the ringleaders arrested. Ohn Kyaw Myint was sentenced to death and executed.

General Tin U, a former chief of staff of the army, was also implicated, although he had not been involved in the abortive coup attempt. He was sentenced to a long prison term. About 200 army officers who were thought to be loyal to Tin U were also questioned and in November 1976 Ne Win himself announced that more than 50,000 BSPP members and cadres had been dismissed from the ruling party. Tin U, one of the most popular army chiefs that Burma has had, was seen as a potential rival and therefore had to be eliminated, along with anyone suspected of being his supporter.

Thoke-thin-ye was put into practice yet again in the early 1980s, and the target this time was not politicians, pro-democracy students or dissident army officers—but Burma's powerful military intelligence apparatus, the main pillar of support for the Ne Win regime.

During his time in Japan with the Thirty Comrades, Ne Win had been specially selected for intelligence training by the dreaded *Kempetai*, the Japanese military police. Its activities in Burma during the Japanese occupation are still remembered by many people who suffered at their hands. The favourite accusation of the *Kempetai* was that a person was a "spy", and that was the word they used in their limited English. Spy or not, confessions were extracted, literally in most cases, by having fingernails, teeth, and hair pulled out.

The savagery, however, was not confined only to such suspects. It was practised even in drilling Burmese cadets. Parade ground bullyings, and reports of fascist terrorism against the population at large, in the end turned most of the Burmese cadets against the Japanese—even if some may have realised that these methods could be quite effective.

The Japanese origins of the Burma Army were largely buried after the war. On 29 August 1947, the defence chief, Bo Let Ya, signed an agreement with the British representative, J.W. Freeman, according to which military equipment and a naval craft would be given to Burma, and a British army, navy, and air force mission would be set up in Burma to assist with the training of the new defence forces. The agreement was eventually abrogated in 1954, but training in Britain continued thereafter on more informal terms.

This training was extended also to members of the intelligence branch. Burma sent promising young men to Britain to receive instruction from not only the Criminal Investigation Department of London's Metropolitan Police Force (Scotland Yard) but also MI6, the British Secret Service. Most of this training took place at the Sheffield Police Academy, and a selected few went to a much more secretive intelligence school called Shetmead.

A man steeped in this tradition was Col. Lwin, nicknamed "Moustache" Lwin because of his impressive handle-bar whiskers. In the 1930s, he had been a *thakin* and a member of the *Dohbama Asiayons* in Pegu Division, where he had clashed with the *Myochit* leader, U Saw. "Moustache" Lwin was still in charge of Burma's

Military Intelligence Service (MIS) when Ne Win seized power in 1962, but before long he was "permitted to retire", as the official term for dismissal goes. His nemesis was Brig.-Gen. Tin U,[1] whose nickname was "Spectacles" Tin U because of the goggle-style glasses he always wore.

Tin U had been trained by the CIA on the Pacific island of Saipan in the 1950s and he was, in effect, Ne Win's adopted son. Ne Win appointed him chief of the MIS in 1972, and his duty was to break with the British tradition and turn the intelligence apparatus into a secret police along the lines of the *Kempetai* or Germany's efficient *Geheime Staatspolizei* (Gestapo), which had been disbanded after the war. The aim was not just to collect necessary military intelligence—which had been Col. Lwin's preoccupation—but to create a secret police that could control the populace. More importantly, it had to check the army to identify and eliminate any possible dissenters within the ranks. If the army turned against Ne Win, he knew he would be finished.

Thus, the *Kempetai* tradition was reborn, hardly by coincidence, at the instigation of someone who had been trained by them. The MIS became a political police organisation that instituted a reign of terror in Burma. The central intelligence office was transferred to Insein Jail, where Tin U supervised the construction of several interrogation centres. The most notorious of these was the *Yay-kyi-aing* ("Clear Water-pond") complex close to Mingaladon airport. Tin U was reported to have taken part, with enthusiasm, in questioning political detainees by torture.

Suspected dissidents were arrested from their homes, usually in the early hours and taken blindfolded to *Yay-kyi-aing* and similar places. Questioning followed under blinding floodlights, and burning cigarettes were stubbed out on naked flesh. Western-style electric shocks were also common, as well as Japanese-inspired water torture.

But Ne Win's second heir apparent suffered the same fate as his predecessor, Aung Gyi—albeit for completely different reasons. Aung Gyi had been somewhat of a "closet liberal" in the context of the hard-line BSPP policies of the early 1960s. The orphan Tin U was a faithful follower of Ne Win, his surrogate father, but in building up the MIS he had become too powerful. His men were the only ones in the country who could travel freely abroad and have access to foreign publications, which they were obliged to read for intelligence purposes.

Ne Win perceived this comparatively enlightened "state within the state" as a potential threat to his own undisputed position as the supreme—and only—ruler of Burma. In May 1983, Tin U was deposed. He was purged along with Col. Bo

Ni, another intelligence chief, and sent to the infamous detention centre that he himself had created, *Yay-kyi-aing*. Hundreds of Tin U's best agents were also dismissed from service. The entire MIS was cut down to size in a process that led to a temporary breakdown in the efficiency of Burma's intelligence services.

The first to take advantage of this were the North Koreans. In October 1983, five months after "Spectacles" Tin U's dismissal, a high-powered South Korean delegation visited Rangoon. On the 9th, they visited the Martyrs' Mausoleum in the capital to pay their respects to Burma's fallen heroes. The South Koreans were waiting for the arrival of their President, Chun Doo Hwan and his wife, when a powerful bomb went off at 10.55 a.m. The middle section of the roof was blown off, sending up a huge mushroom of smoke. The explosion could be heard all over Rangoon and the hundred or so South Korean security guards were seen running out covered with blood.

Fifteen people were instantly killed, among them four cabinet ministers: Deputy Prime Minister for Economic Planning, Shu Suk-Joon; Foreign Minister Lee Bum-Suk; Minister for Commerce and Industry, Kim Dong-Whie; and Minister for Energy and Resources, Suh Sang-Chui. The presidential chief economic secretary also died. Among the twelve injured were Gen. Lee Ki-Back, chairman of the Joint Chiefs of Staff, and five South Korean reporters. The president and his lady—for whom the bomb had been planted—arrived a few minutes late and escaped the devastating blast.

Burmese troops and police immediately began a hunt for the perpetrators. Within a week, two North Korean agents had been captured alive, and one had been killed in an encounter. Justice had been done, and Rangoon was praised internationally—but most observers overlooked the main issue: the bomb blast would not have happened in the first place if Burma's once efficient MIS had not been severely crippled five months before.

Ne Win clearly realised that he had to appoint a new intelligence chief as strong and hard-working as the now imprisoned Tin U had been. The choice was Khin Nyunt, a tactical commander of the 44th Light Infantry Division based along the Karen front in eastern Burma. Khin Nyunt was the perfect choice: a desk officer all his military career, he was virtually a nobody in the Burma Army. He had never seen combat—a rare commodity in the battle-hardened *tatmadaw*. Consequently, he would be extremely thankful for his new position and therefore also unquestionably loyal.

Khin Nyunt's first test in the field came when the entire population of Burma eventually rose up against the military tyranny in 1988. Student protests in March had led to more unrest in June, and in July the BSPP convened an emergency congress. In a curious move, Ne Win announced that he was resigning from his last official post, that of chairman of the BSPP. The new "leader"—as BSPP chairman and President of the Union—was Sein Lwin.

The Burmese public perceived this as a bad joke: Sein Lwin had been a faithful Ne Win loyalist since the days when they both belonged to the 4th Burma Rifles. Moreover, Sein Lwin gained fame when in August 1950 he led the Burma Army unit that managed to track down and kill the leader of the Karen insurgency, Saw Ba U Gyi. Sein Lwin had also led the army units that carried out the massacres of students in Rangoon in July 1962 and in the mid-1970s.

Sein Lwin, "The Butcher", was formally put in charge of suppressing the mass demonstrations of 1988 as well. It was a task in which he failed conspicuously. On 8 August, millions of people across the country took to the streets and demanded an end to military rule. After 26 years of repression, they had had enough. The army responded fiercely from the outset: troops from the 22nd Light Infantry Division were dispatched to disperse the demonstrations with gunfire. At least 3,000 people were killed as the army fired indiscriminately into the crowds of demonstrators.

It was a bloodbath unsurpassed even in BSPP history. The shooting was no accident, nor was it provoked by any of the unarmed protesters. Sein Lwin was simply carrying out his master's orders. When Ne Win had "resigned" in July, he had said in his farewell message: "I have to inform the people throughout the country that when the army shoots, it shoots to kill."

And so it did—but this time to no avail. Despite the massive killings, people from all walks of life kept on marching in the streets of Rangoon, Mandalay, and virtually every town and major village across Burma, from Myitkyina in the northern Kachin Hills to Kawthaung in the far south. Sein Lwin resigned on 12 August after only 18 days as Ne Win's figurehead President.

Then another joker from the pack was selected: the academic lawyer and author, Dr. Maung Maung. The hard-line approach had failed, and a "softer" line was applied. But this did not fool the people: they had had enough of the BSPP regime. Even more people joined the demonstrations: students, Buddhist monks, lawyers, teachers, doctors, farmers, factory workers, and even trishaw paddlers and beggars.

Any government elsewhere in the world would have collapsed in the face of such massive, popular protests, or a compromise would have been reached to solve the crisis. But true to their *thoke-thin-ye* ideal, the Burma Army did not give an inch: instead, the people had to be punished for questioning the military's absolute grip on power.

On 18 September, the chief of the Burma Army, Gen. Saw Maung, stepped in. Dr. Maung Maung was "deposed" in a mock coup. Troops were sent out once again. Moving in perfect formation, they mowed down one group of people after another. Again, scores of people were killed. A new military junta, the State Law and Order Restoration Council (SLORC) was set up over the freshly slaughtered corpses of thousands of unarmed Burmese civilians. An uneasy lull of nine months or so followed.

It was not only the magnitude of the protests, and the massive scale of the killings, that made the 1988 uprising different from those of 1962 and 1974. Before, the protests had been more or less confined to the students. This time, the movement had some very distinguished leaders, who commanded respect from the people. They openly challenged the supreme authority of Ne Win, whose puppets—Sein Lwin, Dr. Maung Maung and now Gen. Saw Maung—had succeeded him in rapid sequence.

One of the first of Burma's old statesmen to go public during the August protest was U Nu, who had returned from exile eight years before. The octogenarian former Prime Minister declared that the coup of 1962 had been illegal and that his government was still the only constitutional one in Burma.

But perhaps even more importantly, Bogyoke Aung San's daughter, Aung San Suu Kyi, emerged as the most popular leader of the pro-democracy movement. When she first appeared at a public meeting on the slopes of the Shwe Dagon Pagoda on 26 August, hundreds of thousands of people showed up. Many were curious to see her because of her famous father, but Aung San Suu Kyi soon established a popularity that was entirely her own: she was courageous and refused to be intimidated by Ne Win's trigger-happy soldiers.

Her very presence was a threat to Ne Win himself: since 1962, he had tried to popularise the myth that he was Aung San's comrade-in-arms who had inherited the army from the slain founder of the *tatmadaw*. Now, Aung San's own daughter was openly challenging Ne Win and his totalitarian rule.

The new MIS chief, Khin Nyunt, was charged with the duty of trying to neutralise her and eliminate the movement that had emerged throughout the country. One of her closest followers was my old friend and colleague Ba Thaw, alias Maung Thawka, a former Lieutenant-Commander of the *Yay Tatmadaw*, or Navy. Already on 31 August, Maung Thawka had written in a personal letter to his

Who Killed Aung San?

friend Capt. Than Nyunt, commander of the Irrawaddy Naval Region: "The army considers Aung San Suu Kyi to be an enemy and is making arrangements to assassinate her . . . in this I have also been designated a target for their death squads." Maung Thawka was arrested a year later and sentenced to 20 years' imprisonment with hard labour. He died in Insein Jail in 1991.

But after the mock coup of September 1988, Aung San Suu Kyi toured the country to meet the people, and was received as a heroine wherever she went. On 5 April 1989, she reached the small town of Danubyu in the Irrawaddy delta region southwest of Rangoon. An army captain, Myint Oo, confronted her with his squad of troops as she and a group of people were walking down a street. The officer then ordered his soldiers to load and take aim at Aung San Suu Kyi. But she bravely went forward alone, after telling her friends to move away to the sides of the road. A major fortunately arrived at the scene and prevented the captain from taking further action. Myint Oo's action was, however, endorsed by the SLORC. He was promoted. The fate of the major is unknown.

The situation was becoming tense, and at a SLORC press conference in Rangoon in early April, Gen. Saw Maung "gave clarification on rumours spread by unscrupulous persons", to quote the official *Working People's Daily* of the 7th. One such so-called rumour was a news item in the Bangkok daily *The Nation* of 2 April: "The latest rumour is that a squad with 30 members has been formed in the Tenasserim Division under the leadership of the government. It is named the Second *Galon* U Saw Group . . . it is fully armed. The task of the squad is to assassinate Aung San Suu Kyi." After achieving its aim, the group was to go underground for some time.

Whatever the case, Aung San Suu Kyi was not shot. But on 20 July 1989, the army surrounded her home on University Avenue in Rangoon and placed her under house arrest. There she remains, by the same lake where Ne Win lives, but on the opposite shore—close to where *Galon* U Saw planned and plotted the assassination of her father. The chairman of the party she had founded, the National League for Democracy (NLD), was also arrested and sentenced to a long prison term. He had been in jail before: he was former army chief, Gen. Tin U, who had also emerged at the fore of the pro-democracy movement of 1988–9.

But despite her detention, Aung San Suu Kyi's popularity did not wane. The military, however, thought that with her out of the way, it would be safe to hold general elections, as Gen. Saw Maung had indeed promised when he "seized power" in September 1988. On 27 May 1990, the Burmese went to the polls. The NLD won an astounding 392 out of 485 contested seats in the assembly. The former BSPP, now renamed the National Unity Party (NUP), secured a mere ten seats. It was a vote against Ne Win and for Aung San Suu Kyi.

The people had spoken—but the army again refused to listen. The assembly was never convened. Instead, more than 60 MPs-elect were arrested, more were "disqualified" on flimsy charges, and about a dozen fled to the Thai border. On 18 December 1990, they set up the National Coalition Government of the Union of Burma led by Dr. Sein Win, the son of U Ba Win, Aung San's elder brother who had also been assassinated on 19 July 1947. Instead of being ruled by a democratically elected government in Rangoon, the Burmese have over the past few years witnessed the rapid rise to power of Ne Win's godson, MIS chief Khin Nyunt, whose hard-liners are consolidating their positions.

It is now 45 years since U Saw's gunmen stormed into the Secretariat and gunned down Aung San and his colleagues. U Saw wiped out his rivals for power, but failed to become the supreme leader himself. Yet his legacy lives on and *thoke-thin-ye* has been practised successfully by Ne Win and his inner circle of cronies ever since the assassination of Aung San. It was not only a national leader that died on that fateful day in July 1947; the decency of the entire nation and its pride in having a functioning democracy were left in tatters.

Even if he did not plot the actual killings, Ne Win is a ruler steeped in the U Saw tradition, while Aung San's daughter Aung San Suu Kyi and his old friend U Nu are trying to continue the work that the national hero began, but was never able to finish, when he was killed at the age of only 32. To most Burmese, Aung San Suu Kyi symbolises what Burma should have been today: peaceful, democratic, and prosperous. Such potential leaders of a free and democratic Burma, which will surely come some day, must not be lost again as we look forward to a happier tomorrow.

7

Postscript

*"All those most valuable leaders together with Bogyoke have
gone from our midst. Like the foam on the river or the bubble in
the fountain all had fallen victims to the dastardly enemy. The
suffering in our hearts is beyond measure"* [1]

Three short essays I had written, about *Galon* Saw's crime and punishment for
the 1947 murders of Burma's top leaders, which appeared in *The Burma Bulletin* [2]
years ago with the headings, "Smile & Smile & be a Villain", "Ghosts, Bananas &
Lemonade", and "Bid Me Despair", drew surprising yet helpful responses which
enhanced the story when I wrote it in book form. The book, in turn, has attracted a
number of queries and comments, some intriguing enough for those interested in
my motherland's modern history, to prompt me to offer some explanations and
recollections.

The Assassination

The review by the noted journalist, Mair Dubois, which appeared in Bangkok's
The Nation, was detailed and insightful. He appeared to base his reflections,
however, on only a few versions proffered by native and foreign writers. Retired
Brigadier Maung Maung's *Burmese Nationalist Movements 1940–48* is quoted as
the veritable source, especially in regard to the part played by U Tun Hla Oung.
The reviewer quotes the following passages from this book:

> p 317. "The cabinet room was U Aung San's own room, one floor directly above the
> office of DIG CID [Deputy Inspector General, Head of the Criminal Investigations
> Department of Burma Police]. Newspapers the next day reported that there were two
> Europeans, army officers, present in the DIG CID room at the time who drove away in
> a jeep immediately after the shootings. Later they were identified as Brigadier Nash,

Commander South Burma District [of the Burma Command] and Brigadier Knight, the BGS (Int) [Brigadier General Staff, Intelligence] of Headquarters Burma Command."

p 321. "The surprising thing was that the head of the CID seemed to know what was going on and whom to arrest as soon as the event had occurred. The DIG CID U Tun Hla Oung, took the IGP into Bogyoke Aung San's room within minutes of the shootings; before the day wore out he had led a police posse (BAPS, a para-military military force formed from the PVOs, a substitute for the pre-war BMP, the Burma Military Police, manned almost exclusively with Indian Muslims from the Punjub and Frontier Provinces and led by British Officers seconded from the British regiments) into U Saw's compound."

p 339: Note 124 "A few minutes after the assassins had left the building, U Tun Hla Oung, DIG CID, went from his room to IGP's, said he had heard a commotion in the room above, that they should go and check, went up and saw the disaster."

Mair Dubois mentioned that I had not taken "the opportunity to respond to claims" regarding "my fathers role" in the sequences related above. The references had been based, it appears, on local newspapers reports. This was admittedly so in regard to references to the "two European army officers", which were published the day after the killings. News gathered in those tumultuous times resulted in reporting a mixture of fact and fabrication. Among the popular assumptions were that the British Imperialists had fomented the plot; that Burmese politicians had been manipulated by them; and that top native civil servants had been culpable because of their allegedly pro-British inclinations. The ferocity of the attacks by the media against those three categories increased in scale from the Right to the Left, with the Communists being the most virulent in their newspapers such as *The Communist Daily.* The assertions were particularly inflamed and wild immediately after the assassinations.

The four *Galon* assassins broke into the Council Chamber in the mid-morning of 19 July 1947, and fired their automatic weapons at the occupants for thirty seconds. The sound of gun-fire had been likened to that made by a collapsing building, to the explosion of a dozen grenades, and also to the barking of automatic weapons of large calibre.

The room next door was that of the Bogyoke's aide, Bo Tun Hla, and Lieut. Than Win (aide-de-camp to the General Officer Commanding, Burma Command) was visiting him. They fell flat on the floor when the guns went off but rose quickly and Bo Tun Hla rushed into the chamber, followed by his friend. They were the first to arrive (chapter 1, p 12). U Tin Ohn, the assistant secretary of the Council who had seen the armed thugs come up the stairway, was the next person to enter that room.

U Ba Maung, the Inspector-General of Police, was presiding over a senior civil police officers' meeting which had started in the same building at 9 a.m. on that Saturday morning. The Commissioner of Police, Rangoon City, U Aung Chein, and DIG CID U Tun Hla Oung were there. At 10.30 a.m. they were startled by the explosions, which the Commissioner described on the witness stand as "falling bricks", and later to my father as "a rumbling noise". The meeting ended then.

The police offices were located in the eastern wing of the double-storeyed Secretariat. Government offices occupied the east, south and west connected buildings, with a smaller section on the north-side, facing the requisitioned St. Paul's school occupied by the navy, making the fourth side of the square complex. The last building included the living quarters allocated to junior staff and a post office. The IGP's office itself, on the ground floor of the east-wing, was almost directly opposite the Bogyoke's. This room on the first floor on the west side, had detachable walls and was expanded to serve as the Council Chamber.

When the Special Tribunal began its hearing of the witnesses, Commissioner Aung Chein, as the formal complainant in the case, was the first to appear on the prosecution's side. He deposed that he had walked from the IGP's room to the west wing and when he reached the Council Chamber he found Bo Tun Hla and Tin Ohn there.

Tun Hla Oung was prosecution witness No. 38. He was well known as a man of action. He drove his car to the western area, moving out of the south-west exit gate to Sparks Street, and questioned everyone in sight. Making no headway he returned through the north-west gate. The IGP, U Ba Maung, had by then learnt about the shootings, and as soon as Tun Hla Oung returned he reported to him and they both went at once to the scene of the carnage. They then proceeded to the office of the Chief Secretary, U Ka Si, to advise him of the tragedy. Tun Hla Oung was still in conference with the Chief Secretary when the telephone call came from Capt. Khan. The captain was asked to come to the Secretariat and he made a personal report to the CID Chief when he reached him within the half hour.

The two European army officers mentioned by Maung Maung in his book were "identified as Brigadier Nash, Commander South Burma District [of the Burma Command] and Brigadier Knight, the BGS (Int) [Brigadier General Staff, Intelligence] of Headquarters Burma Command." They "drove away in a jeep immediately after the shootings." Incidentally, this central paragraph in page 317, is often quoted in the military regimes' media, usually around Martyrs' Day. It will also be relevant to quote Note No. 125, p 339, which the author had published as the reference to this context:

> Brigadier Nash was the elder brother of P.G.E. Nash, ICS, the principal Secretary of the Governor's own Secretariat within the Government House. In Telm. Gvr.-SSB, No. 313 of 28th July, in para. 6. "On 18th July I visited Philip Nash in hospital and found that he knew of the loss of arms . . . gave me additional information that British officers (afterwards discovered to be Hunt the DS [Defence Security Officer, Lt.Col. Hunt of HQ Burma Command]) had been watching Saw's bungalow at night with field glasses and had seen Saw with four or five men in a boat in somewhat suspicious circumstances on several occasions. Saw, . . . always well dressed . . . presumed . . . that . . . case of woman" Nash then warned him of Army Staff's belief that Saw stocking up a large quantity of arms. This was prior to the actual assassination. Hunt was an employee in a business firm in pre-War Rangoon and had known Saw's predilections . . . . The DIG CID had also posted a watch on U Saw's house to gather intelligence from across the Lake. See Saw trial police CID witness's deposition."

Another story circulating at the time was that Sir Nick Lamour, Deputy-Secretary to Sir Hubert Rance, was working in his office below that of the council chamber when the murders took place. This takes us to another statement ascribed to Philip Nash[3], as follows:

> Another facet to this macabre story is that, until about a week before the assassination, two British NCOs seconded to the Burma Police were on duty at the entrance steps leading up to the Council Chamber when the Council was in session. This offended the "amour propre" of the Burmese and the NCOs were withdrawn. It is for conjecture as to what might have happened if these NCOs had been in position on the 19th. They were armed and would not have been so easily taken in by the old 12th Army uniforms worn by the assassins.

Philip Nash's words actually contradicted some of the material contained in the Acting Governor's Secretary R.W.D. Fowler's telegram to Sir Gilbert Laithwaite, sent at 16.25 hrs on 19 July (p 110 Appendix). In a message which is full of inaccuracies, Fowler had said that the jeep which the perpetrators had arrived in had carried 12th Army markings, but in fact the hitmen had been identified by the armed PVO standing guard outside the Chamber door, who had been badly wounded by them, as 4th Burma Rifles personnel.

The peon Thaung Sein who had stood at the door of the Council room had worn jungle-green trousers. Ko Htwe, U Razak's youthful bodyguard, who rushed out from a room close by on hearing the firing and was shot, was dressed in an army type uniform and probably carried a pistol. The latter must have been mistaken for a PVO sentinel. The 4th Burma Rifles was Ne Win's battalion.

That security was lax on that fateful day is undeniable. It was like any other working day, although perhaps less security conscious since Saturdays were then "half-holidays", as we referred to them. Everything was quite casual then. The British NCOs posted, when the Governor's Council was meeting, at the bottom of the stairway leading up to the Chamber, appear to have been mainly ceremonial. There were many other approaches to Bogyoke's office. The reason put forward for the withdrawal of the foreign guards, that it was because the "amour propre" of the Burmese had been offended, may have been true. There was believed to be a police unit permanently stationed in the complex for maintenance of security. It is known that a policeman had unsuccessfully ordered the driver of the assassins' jeep, when he drove up to the foot of the stairway ready for the get-away, to move on, just as the guns went off. There were some Councillors who kept aides or bodyguards and Bo Tun Hla and Ko Htwe were around at the time. Apart from those few precautions, which in the aftermath look woefully inadequate, the Secretariat in those days was virtually "- *ta-ga ma-shi:dah ma-shi*" literally, "no gate: no sword"! The main gates were wide open, letting through motor vehicles and pedestrians in office hours. This easy access was clearly demonstrated by U Saw's advance reconnaissance party and his gunmen in their jeep.

Another significant aspect of the deficiency in safety precautions was that the leader Bogyoke, Aung San himself had felt "secure in the affections of his people." This was a reference to the majority of the people of Burma; he was averse to ostentation and considered that he needed no special protection—at work, at home, or anywhere he went.

Yet it was a time of imminent danger. Large quantities of arms and ammunition had been pilfered from British army stores. On 15 July, Bogyoke himself, accompanied by Pyawbwe U Mya, the acting Home Councillor, had gone to the Governor to report the finding of a suspicious issue of Bren guns and spare parts. It had occurred on 24 June, and Aung San had then expressed to Sir Hubert his anxiety, particularly about the considerable time lag between the actual loss and its discovery. This extremely serious matter had been brought to the attention of top officials only the day before (chapter 4, pp 53 & 54). Three days later, and a day before the assassination, Thakin Nu went to report to Sir Hubert of an Army Depot issue of a great quantity of ammunition to unknown persons. Following the Bogyoke's meeting with the Governor, local newspapers gave the news front-page treatment.

It was understood that Aung San and his government had on the agenda of the last Council meeting on 19 July, a plan to prepare a firm and prompt action against the perpetrators of the arms thefts. It was believed that a raid on U Saw's residence was in fact being scheduled to take place as early as within forty-eight hours from the time of the meeting.

The investigations into the thefts were conducted by the Criminal Investigations Department of the Burma Police, in coordination with that of the Commissioner of Police, Rangoon. The British Burma Command's Intelligence were also working on the case, but it is not known how closely they had cooperated with the Burma Police. The CID had posted watchers on U Saw's home from 17 July, and Capt Khan, Saw's neighbour, had participated in the surveillance. It was Khan's report to Tun Hla Oung that inspired the planned strike at the *Galon* base of operations. Following the capture of the "headquarters" of the *Galons,* with their "general" and the assassination teams, houses of other political leaders like Dr Ba Maw and Thakin Ba Sein were raided; an estimated 800 people found themselves in custody in the weeks that followed. There is nothing "surprising" about Tun Hla Oung, DIG CID, doing his job and doing it very well at that. His regular army training and years of service in the military and civil police had honed his natural skills to the top of his bent.

Inheriting a family tradition of patriotism, but quite apolitical, he gave his loyalty to legitimate authority and performed his duties without fear nor favour. There were quite a few like him among Burmese civil and military services personnel at the time and although they were at first looked upon with suspicion by young nationalists for their alleged pro-British tendencies, many of them came to be accepted for what they were worth: U Tun Hla Oung and my father-in-law Justice Thaung Sein, were two officials who gained the confidence of leading nationalists, including the Minister for Home and Judicial Affairs U Kyaw Nyein, the socialist king-pin.

Mysterious Trio:

Readers of the first edition of my book who were captivated by some of the characters mentioned such as Bingley, Saw Sein Hmon and Malhotra.

John Stewart Bingley, British Council representative, had featured in the book as the mysterious "tall gentleman" (chapter 4, pp 52–54 & pp 56–58), and the question posed at the end of that chapter is—"Who exactly was Bingley?".

Bingley's involvement with U Saw has received only cursory mention by writers, but he seems to have gone out of his way to ally himself with forces against Aung San and his friends. They represented to him, and to his kind, a threat to the interests of the British Empire. Major Young introduced Bingley to U Saw at one of the parties thrown by the latter in his home. According to Young, Bingley had declared at his very first meeting with the *Galon* chief, in a voice loud enough for everyone to hear, that they were all ready to be of complete help to him. He was mentioned once and fleetingly by Sir Ba U[4] in his autobiography *My Burma,* but it is relevant enough to be noteworthy. He had been in the company of a senior civil servant known to be an incorrigible British Imperialist, out to thwart Burmese Nationalist programmes by every means.

It was suspicious that Bingley had wanted to make the acquaintance of a Burman of influence, who, they both must have imagined, could be swayed to their machinations. Sir Ba U's narration of the occurrence, sometime in 1947, is as follows:

"while we were still in the middle of the drafting of the Constitution. It had a considerable bearing on the rising of the Mons and Karens. One day at 5.30 p.m. a senior civilian named Donald Burman Petch called on me in my house in Golden Valley. The visit was very unexpected. Though I knew the man, I had not seen him for a number of years. We were once together in Myaungmya, where he was the Deputy Commissioner when I was the Sessions Judge. We had not met since my promotion to the High Court in 1930. At the time of the visit he was the commissioner of the Tenasserim Division. After exchanging a few preliminary remarks Petch said, 'Ba U, you are now going to get independence, and I understand that you are going to have a federal form of Government. Why don't you persuade your young friends to give the Tenasserim Division as a State to the Karens? There can be keen competition between the Karens and the Burmans. They can make Moulmein their main port and you can make Rangoon your main port. Progress lies in competition.

I was terribly angry at this and said, 'You are talking like a child. You must understand that the Karens form a minority while the Burmans form a majority; in the Tenasserim Division. Besides the Burmans, there are the Mons. You can't expect a minority to rule the majority; there would soon be trouble. We have, however, already made a provision in our Constitution to give a state to the Karens. You must understand, Petch, that we are more generous than you are. Though the Scotch and the Welsh have been demanding Home Rule for years, you have refused to give it to them. What you suggest would cause trouble between the Karens and the Burmans. I am glad to know that there are very few Englishmen like you. Now, will you go. My time for dinner is past. I am hungry, I can't ask you to stay to dinner because there is none for you.'

He got up and left saying, 'I will come again to continue the discussion.'

A few days later he did come with a man called J.S. Bingley, Representative of the British Council in Rangoon. I refused to see them."

A friend whom I had not heard from for well nigh forty years wrote from Tucson, Arizona, USA, to tell me that he knew Sein Hmon (chapter 5, p 68), in 1949-50. "Our Rangoon Correspondent" who wrote the article "Who really killed Aung San?" in the Karen National Bulletin of April 1986, had conferred the Karen prefix of *Saw* on him, but he had simply gone by the name of U Sein Hmon, when he was my friend's neighbour in Lower Kemmendine Road in Rangoon. He was under suspension from government service at the time, but my correspondent does not know whether he was in the civil police and, if so, whether he was in charge of the Insein district in July 1947. However, my friend wrote:

I distinctly remember U Sein Hmon as a taciturn person of integrity and cannot imagine that he would invent or fabricate a story about having arrested U Saw moments before Aung San and his colleagues were mowed down, unless it really happened that way. I wonder if the KNU Rangoon correspondent ever interviewed U Sein Hmon personally or whether U Sein Hmon was still alive in 1986, when the article was written. It could very well be that the 'correspondent' got only a second-hand story about U Sein Hmon's involvement in the U Saw's case.

Another possible aspect of this story is that following Capt. Khan's personal report to my father, the Inspector-General of Police, the Chief Secretary, the Rangoon Commissioner of Police and he had determined on the arrest of U Saw. The raid was assigned to U Aung Chein, the Commissioner, but he was hesitant and asserted that Ady Road, where U Saw resided, was in Insein district jurisdiction. That may have been when U Sein Hmon, as District Superintendent of Police of Insein, if in fact he held that post at the time, was alerted.my own understanding is that the DIG CID had advised against procrastination and took on the responsibility himself.

As for Malhotra (chapter 4, p 55 & chapter 5.p 64) of Leele & Co., he was an Indian businessman who had lived in the Fytche Flats, where David Vivian was also a tenant. Malhotra might have been a front for certain British commercial firms, who was useful to them to keep up their connections with U Saw. He probably desired to ingratiate himself with the politicians who might have a pivotal role in the future. Malhotra and his wife, continued to live in Rangoon, were seen at social functions years later. Mrs. Malhotra was active in a Burmese Womens' maternity and welfare association.

Son of Sao Sam Htun:

Of the descendants of the leaders martyred in July 1947, the most famous at present is, of course, the daughter of the Bogyoke himself, Aung San Suu Kyi who was then a baby. After reading my story another of the offspring has come forward to tell me what he could remember.

He is Sao Sai Hom, son of Sao Sam Htun, who was twelve years old, studying at St. Ann's Convent, a co-educational institution at Taunggyi, with his younger brother and two sisters, when they heard the shocking news over the radio. His mother and another sister had passed away earlier and the boys were boarding with (Air Commodore) Tommy Clift's mother. The four orphaned and distraught children started out to travel down to Rangoon by train but were held up for a whole week en route at Thazi junction because the monsoon rains had flooded the tracks.

In the capital city, they were looked after by Sao Hkun Hkio, Sawbwa of Mong Mit, who became the Republic's first Foreign Minister. Taken to see the Martyrs lying in state in the Jubilee Hall, Sao Sai Hom noticed that his father's body, resting in a glass casket, had special trappings of loyalty, befitting his princely status.

When Sao Sam Htun's remains were conveyed to his state capital of Mong Pawn by train, a motor cavalcade had to complete the journey from Shwe Nyaung, the terminus, on a drive of about forty-four miles. Traditional ceremonies were observed there. On the final day, many Sawbwas of other states, dignitaries and thousands of people attended the cremation. Sao Sai Hom, as the eldest son, lit the funeral pyre. He recollected that the body incinerated very quickly. The ashes were then gathered and entombed.

Who Killed Aung San?

Years later, Sao Sai Hom was told by a doctor, who was present at the Rangoon General Hospital when the dead and dying were brought there on that fateful day, that Sawbwagyi Sao Sam Htun managed to murmur a few words in brief snatches of consciousness—"Look after the others," he said, "they are more hurt than I." He died the next day.

Nasty, Racist Murder?

Dr. Gehan Wijeyewardene, Ph.D., of the Australian National University, pp 24–27, the following question has asked in his review of my book in the Thai-Yunnan Project Newsletter No. 23, December 1994 :

> There comes a point when questions have to be asked about the Burmese leadership of our time. The symbol of Aung San is a necessary one, but was he without fault? There are suggestions that the British warrant for his arrest on his return from the meetings of the Indian National Congress, the warrant that had led to his escape and journey to Amoy, was not for political offences but for a particularly nasty, racist murder.

Was he (Bogyoke Aung San) without fault?

Put this question personally to a Burman-Buddhist and the response will invariably be *"Kyoke ka Phaya-laung hma ma hoke ta"*: literally, "Not being the future Buddha myself", as Aung San himself might have answered it. This natural expression, is, to most of us, simply meant to convey that because one is but a mere mortal the immaculate state of the Exalted One is yet myriad years away. But even in the Buddhist philosophy of cause and effect, as pointed out by U Nu after his friend's untimely death, "the Bogyoke did not easily attain that peak of prestige and influence." U Nu added: "He earned it by his sacrifice, his integrity, his humility, his dedication, his patriotism, his courage. These sterling qualities he consistently showed throughout his life, and in the result the people responded with their love and trust". And so, Aung San had his faults but the Burmese nonetheless loved and trusted him and maintain, in the words of Oliver Goldsmith—*"We must touch his weaknesses with a delicate hand. There are some faults so nearly allied to excellence, that we can scarce weed out the fault without eradicating the virtue."*[5]

The question, however, remains. Could Aung San's weaknesses have led him to engage in homicide "a particularly nasty, racist" one?

Six days after the declaration of war by Great Britain and France on Germany on 3 September 1939, the *Dohbama Asiayone* published a detailed policy statement which had had been decided at a conference in Tharawaddy—incidentally, the birthplace of *Galon* Saw. It contained nine cardinal points which in essence offered Burmese cooperation provided certain demands were complied with and virtually asked for independence as soon as preparations were completed. The Government chose to overlook the overture but the awakening of the nationalists to the unique opportunity of using the global conflict to gain freedom appealed to the public. The idea spread rapidly, fanned by political leaders who took their resolutions to the people. In October 1939, the two major organisations, Dr Ba Maw's *Sinyetha Wunthanu Aphwe*—Nationalist Proletarian Party—and *Dohbama Asiayone* and other organisations formed the national united front of the Burma Freedom Bloc, with Dr Ba Maw as the president and Thakin Aung San as secretary-general. The latter and a small group of friends called the Burma Revolutionary Party (BRP) of underground revolutionaries were active.

In March 1940, Thakin Aung San attended the Ramgardh Session of the Indian National Congress. On his return, with the war in Europe rapidly deteriorating for the Allies, the Governor of Burma was confronted with anti-British civil disobedience campaigns, and with threats by the nationalist groups to impede the war effort, unless they were promised independence. The Defence of Burma Act was brought in to suppress the dissidents. Most prominent Thakins and other politicians were rounded up, tried for sedition and thrown into jail. Many were sentenced to twelve months imprisonment but detained beyond that. Thakin Nu and Dr Ba Maw were successively arrested on 4 and 10 July.

Meanwhile, Aung San had spoken to a rally at Zalun, in the Irrawaddy Division not far from Tharawaddy, in his inimitably forthright manner, challenging Sir Archibald Cochrane, the Governor, to attempt to counteract the man who had become his chief antagonist. The Henzada District Superintendent of Police issued a warrant for his arrest and, typical of Eurasian officials of the time, denigrated him by adding a paltry monetary reward for his capture. Thakin Aung San went underground. On 8 August he slipped out of the country with a companion, Thakin Hla Myaing, with 200 Rupees and a vision. He eventually emerged leading an army as Bo Teza, alias Major-General Omoda, alias Bogyoke Aung San.

Throughout the above period, from the beginning of World War II to the departure of Aung San, patriotic young Thakins and students and certain politicians had set aside their differences and presented a united front in the struggle to shed British Imperialism. Thakin Aung San had selflessly and boldly taken a leading part in the patriotic activities which were quite free of racial overtones. Referring particularly to the four months or so between Aung San's return from India till he went to China, there is no documentation or hint of his having killed anyone. The records of the Government of the day establish that Aung San was wanted only for political agitation and anti-war propaganda, which were tantamount to sedition under the law.

Since the allegation of a heinous crime committed by Aung San lacks substantiation, how did it ever originate? It must be presumed that the misapprehension occurred through the wrong conclusions being drawn by a researcher of the Burma Office records. He may have come across British-Burma Government's telegrams of November 1945, concerning claims that Aung San had committed such a murder. Those messages had wrongly reported the year of the alleged crime as 1932! The date was subsequently corrected.

More questions then arise. Could it have been that reference to a "racist murder" was anachronistic, in that it did happen but at a later date? If so, was it "racist", and was the crime "murder"? In trying to find the answers one will have to go back to early 1946. It was on 28 February of that year, at the first session of the Legislative Council, that Thakin Tun Oke rose and accused Aung San of killing a village headman near Thaton during the advance northwards of the main force of the Burma Independence Army. Aung San at the time held the rank of Major-General and Senior Staff Officer, junior only to two Japanese officers. Tun Oke proposed that Aung San should be placed under arrest and tried, and that having been an eye witness to the murder he was willing to give evidence at the trial.

The Government had had an earlier confidential police report regarding the incident but Councillor Tun Oke's statement was the first public announcement. The British Governor at this time, Sir Reginald Dorman-Smith, seized on the charges as means to stultify Aung San. Dorman-Smith telegraphed the Secretary of State for Burma in London for approval to arrest him, but he was against immediate arrest since investigations were still proceeding. A meeting was convened at Government House in Rangoon on 27 March, to prepare a submission to Sir Reginald on what should be done, but the top military and police officers, and administrative officers, predicted a rebellion if Aung San were taken into custody, while the civilian officials felt that such action would actually head it off. Then Lord Mountbatten interceded, to the annoyance of the Governor, by transmitting a secret cipher message to the Secretary (27/3) reading:

Although I have no longer any responsibility for Burma I still have a close interest in its future as the result of my period of Military Governorship. I am therefore most disturbed at this proposal to arrest Aung San. If the case referred to by Tun Oke is the case you mentioned to me it is a matter of opinion whether it is a case of murder or not.The incident in question is now four years old and I should have thought our best policy would have been to forget incidents of this sort in which there are conflicting opinions. Aung San's "antics" may be disturbing but there is no doubt in my mind that he played the game by me and in view of his youth he is bound to be a leading figure for years to come. In my opinion we would do better to concentrate on showing him and his friends the paths in which we think the true future of Burma lies. I therefore wish to go on record that I consider the arrest of Aung San at the present time the greatest disservice which could be done towards the future relationship of Burma within the British Empire.

In April, Ma Ahma, wife of the *thugyi* (headman) who lost his life, filed a petition with the Military Secretary to the Governor. It was dated 8 April, and was not publicised at the time. The *thugyi's* name was Abdul Raschid and he was headman of Thebyugone village, located in Paung Township of Thaton District. She stated that her husband had:

joined the service as Headman of the Thebyugone village about 25 years ago after the death of his father U Ya Shin who was the *thugyi* of the said village. That during his tenure as the Headman of Thebyugone village he was very faithful to the British Government having discharged his duties to the fullest satisfaction of his superiors and a reference to U Ba San, the ADC of Moulmein will testify to it. Further when the Thakin movement started giving various sort of troubles to the British Administration, the petitioner's husband was working day and night to suppress all uprising within his jurisdiction and this fact was well known to Thakhin Aung San, now General Aung San, before he went to Japan to fight against the Britishers.

She went on to describe her husband's arrest in 1942 by Thakin Aung San and his "confederates".This took place soon after the British evacuation of the Thaton District in the face of the Japanese advance from Martaban. Her husband, she said, was tied with ropes and taken to Thaton town in a bullock-cart where he was confined for eight days without food. He was then taken to the football [soccer] ground and, in the presence of thousands of people, speared him to death with his bionet (sic) after crucifying him to the goal post". She maintained that British law did not differentiate between the rich and the poor and pleaded that "Thakhin Aung San may be dealt with according to the Law." And signed her name as "Ma Ma", in Burmese, as the Petitioner, care-of Kunji Mohd. Kaka of Paung.

Bogyoke Aung San took it upon himself to explain his stand in an article published in the *Thadinsone* (Complete News) *Journal* on 12 April. It was in the vernacular and an English translation appeared in the *Hanthawaddy*. In referring to the accusations levelled at him by Thakin Tun Oke his rebuttal read:

> In the case characterised as murder, the headman of a certain village was sentenced to death for offences with which he had been charged by the villagers. I cannot fully recollect the name of the headman or the village or the particular nature of the offences he was said to have committed. All that I remember is that the headman was a wicked person who ill-treated his villagers and was kept in the custody of the Burma Independence Army (BIA) which first arrived in the Thaton District.
>
> At that time I and another person (the one now accusing me) [Thakin Tun Oke] happened to be in that locality coming down from the North to collect new recruits for the BIA and to get personnel for administering a provisional national government. At Thaton I instituted a Peace Preservation Committee and at the time I came to learn of four or five people being placed under arrest for offences committed in that district. I also learnt that there was one clear case in which villagers concerned had arrested and placed in the custody of the BIA, their own headman. It was also reported to me that the offences he committed merit no less a punishment than death. So I said, "in this case, he must be killed" and I executed the accused.

A meeting then took place between Aung San and Dorman-Smith. Sir Reginald reported the discussions to the Secretary in a telegram of 25 May 1946. A part of the relevant item #6, is quoted below:

> He [Aung San] said that he reached a certain village and heard lurid stories of how the headman was treating the villagers and oppressing them. Those were days of rough justice. The country was in an absolutely lawless condition. There were no courts or magistrates. Having considered the case, and bearing in mind the need for immediate action in order to restore some semblance of authority, he decided that the man must die. As this was his own decision, he felt it incumbent to carry out the execution.

Even earlier, towards the end of 1945, the Commander-in-Chief of the Burma Command had submitted the file to the Supreme Allied Commander Southeast

Asia, Admiral Lord Louis Mountbatten, who had returned it with his comments. A remark read, "in the unsettled conditions which must have existed, it was only to be expected, I suppose, that summary justice would rule, and that old scores would be paid off."

Here one has three versions of the ostensible motive for the killing. First, the stories about mistreatment of villagers by their headman justified the death penalty which was carried out to restore order; second, that he had zealously served British interests in suppressing the Thakin movement in his area; and, third, the killing was paying off old scores. Based on available information, I would venture to make the inference that probably all three played their part.

I myself remember an eye-witness (not Tun Oke) telling me that Abdul Raschid's crime and punishment were widely promulgated in Thaton town days before the event and the public were invited to witness the execution. On that day, the eye-witness had seen that, the prisoner was indeed tied to a goal post of the soccer field. BIA personnel were lined up before him. A man in officers' uniform struck the first blow. The weapon used was a bayonet, attached to the muzzle of a rifle, and the fatal stabbing was taken as if in training on a bag of straw. The officer seemed to have ordered the nearest soldier to strike a similar blow. He promptly obeyed the order and the man was bayoneted again and again.

A pool of blood soaked into the parched earth as the crowd dispersed and the corpse was removed. Only the scars on the wooden goal post remained, and soon the soccer ball was being kicked around the field.

Had Aung San Lived?

I have left a leading, albeit hypothetical, question till the last:

If Aung San had not been killed, would the course of Burma have been different?

Analysts, both indigenous and foreign, have presented their views on this question in their writings on the period immediately before Burma's independence. Almost all agree that he was a good and great man. To the Burmese, in particular, he is their national hero of the century.

Biographers have presented the life of this charismatic and complex personality in academic works. Bogyoke Aung San's proverbial patriotism, courage, zeal, charisma and many other laudable attributes, which endeared him to his people and brought acclaim from the rest of the world, would have been tested had he lived longer, in time and age. The goal of all his endeavours was reached on 4

January 1948, and it would have been his immense task to ensure a glorious future for the new republic.

Leaving aside Bogyoke Aung San's nationalistic university student days, followed by his Marxist initiation into politics, the relevant starting point to this question could be the final talks in Kandy, which started on 6 September 1945, between the Supreme Allied Commander Lord Louis Mountbatten and his staff and the Bogyoke and his delegation. The expeditious disbandment of the Burma National Army, then called the Patriotic Burma Forces, was agreed upon, and resulted in their re-enlistment in the regular battalions of the British Army. The meeting had been cordial and at their parting Mountbatten counselled Aung San, "You must decide to be either a Churchill or a Wellington. You cannot be a soldier and a political leader at the same time." He also handed him a note.

Towards the end of the month, the Bogyoke (this was perhaps the last time this official term was to be formally used) replied to the Supreme Allied Commander's note. It had contained an offer of a commission in the new Army, in the rank of a Brigadier, and appointment to the position of "Burmese" Deputy Inspector-General. He wrote, inter alia:

'I have placed before my colleagues in the AFPFL and the PBF your offer to appoint me in the Burma Army. Although we need to put this matter through some procedures before a decision is recorded, I can say now that I shall be giving up the military career. I regret very much that I shall not be able to serve further in the Army, but this is the majority decision and I must abide by it." That was when he nominated Bo Let Ya, not Bo Ne Win, to that top "Burmese" position in the armed forces. At the same time, he requested consideration to the appointment of Colonel Kya Doe "the most senior Karen officer in the regular Burma Army" to take the place of Bo Let Ya's "colleague". He also expressed his "sincere appreciation and gratitude for what you have done for us in the Southeast Asia war that has just ended." Expressing hope "to retain the happy relations" he presented him with a Japanese Samurai dagger.

When Aung San took off his British-style general's uniform, having cast aside the Japanese one before then, he was once more comfortable in national dress, which Burmese men and women wear with pride to this day. The transformation— from an inspired and singularly patriotic youth to an army veteran and then on to an adept politician and, finally, moving into the last stage of a mature statesman— had begun. The count-down to the end was then just about 662 days: time was running out and there was so much for him to do.

A month before the Bogyoke had informed Lord Mountbatten that he was leaving the army, the Anti-Fascist Peoples' Freedom League had been formed under Aung San's leadership and the League became the predominant political organisation in the country. A major constituent of the AFPFL was the Socialist Party and it soon established itself as the most influential component. Socialism was then adopted as the ideology of the League.

The political situation picked up momentum and the year 1946 was replete with mass meetings, demonstrations and strikes. Lawlessness was rampant in the countryside. The Governor, Sir Reginald Dorman-Smith, left mid-year and Major-General Sir Hubert E. Rance succeeded him. The negotiation and successful conclusion of the Aung San-Attlee Agreement bridged the years 1946-1947. The goal of independence within one year was about to be realised. Burmese political leaders had sought independence in tandem with economic advancements. They wished to terminate the colonial type of economy and replace it with a new socialist system, with emphasis on nationalisation and industrialisation.

It was as Deputy Chairman of the Governor's Council that the Bogyoke attended the annual general meeting of the Burma Chamber of Commerce on 27 February 1947 in Rangoon. He addressed the Chamber, in reply to the Chairman's speech, and his declaration on socialisation is of interest—"I stand for the ultimate nationalisation of all industries. I firmly believe that only nationalisation can give higher standards of living and greater happiness to the peoples." . . . "I do not believe that capitalism is desirable for all time. But I also hold the view that in this country like Burma we have yet to go through the capitalist phase before we can advance further.'

April saw elections to the Constituent Assembly, won almost completely by the AFPFL. The entire League was inundated with national tasks and members were selected to serve on committees to determine major projects. In the third week of May, the League appointed a committee to prepare a draft of the constitution. The committee did so in time for the Constituent Assembly to take it over when it began its session from 10 June. The draft submitted featured an independent sovereign republic of a national union devoted to democracy and socialism. Six days later, Aung San moved a resolution adopting seven basic principles of the new constitution, which was debated on and later accepted.

Bogyoke Aung San was everywhere. He presided over the constitution drafting committee and concurrently dealt in planning for the rehabilitation of the country. He convened at the Sorrento Villa on 6 June, a national conference to draw up, as exhorted in his inaugural speech, simple and practical yet flexible and not over-ambitious plans. He recommended a host of proposals and requirements, including encouragement of cooperatives and securing people's cooperation.

Time was slipping by much too swiftly and then there were just six days left.

In a speech, which many have interpreted as being portentous, he spoke to the public at his last meeting on 13 July, in the City Hall Rangoon, reporting on the progress of the Constituent Assembly and giving his thoughts on the future of his country.

"Independence is coming," he admonished, "but it is not going to bring a heaven on earth. Some of you may dream fondly that once we are independent, there will not be the need to work, and the good things will sprout out of the earth to take as you wish. That is not so. Years of toil lie ahead of you. Maybe 20 years at the least, will past before you see the fruits of your toil".

That meeting on 13 July, had been presided over by Thakin Nu, the president of the Constituent Assembly, who had headed a Goodwill Mission to the United Kingdom and returned just the day before. It was fitting that *Kogyi* (elder brother) Nu succeeded Aung San, and he inherited the latter's endeavours and accomplishments. The constitution was officially adopted on 24 September,

Prior to independence, a Ministry of National Planning had been organised and in April 1948, as the result of the "Sorrento Villa" conference, an outline "Two-Year Economic Development Plan" was made known. In building a social democratic welfare state in a parliamentary democracy, industrial development by state planning was envisaged and nationalisations soon followed. Sensibilities and biases, however, impeded the nationalisation processes and the other economic steps taken by U (he dropped the Thakin prefix in 1952) Nu and his colleagues during the ten years from 1948, when he presided over a coalition government of diverse factions. History credits U Nu with some achievements in reconstruction, as well as in reconciliation, guided by the Socialist ideology, tempered by his own philosophy of liberalism and Buddhism.

Whether or not Aung San's *Lanzin* (Way) could have produced better results if the Bogyoke himself had been at the helm to bring his Socialist theories into realisation is speculative and debatable. It may be that the strain of attempting implementation of a State Socialism system itself put the building of the Welfare State beyond the capabilities of a democratic government.

When General Ne Win, claiming to be Aung San's heir, usurped power in March 1962, he had claimed that the weak and inefficient parliamentary democracy system had to be swept away. He imagined that authoritarianism was best suited to promote unity and rapid economic growth. The origin and purpose of his single-party creation the *Myanma Socialist Lanzin* Party or the Burma Socialist Programme Party (BSPP) was stated to be:

> The Revolutionary Council of the Union of Burma, having rescued the Union, not a moment too soon, from utter disintegration, now strives to reconstruct the social and economic life of all citizens by the Burmese Way to Socialism.

The Constitution adopted by the Revolutionary Council on 4 July 1962, stipulated in Section 18, that the party as a whole was pledged to carry out the Burmese Way to Socialism to "strive towards the establishment of a Socialist Economy."

That was the beginning of the end.

And so, once again, the people were forced to swallow the laxative of this system which plunged the nation into the depths of ignominy. In October 1987, with foreign exchange reserves at virtually zero and foreign debt at US$ 4.4 billion, the United Nations approved the Ne Win government's humble appeal to grant them the beggarly status of Least Developed Country (LDC) on 29 October.

After almost forty years of experimenting in socialism, first under parliamentary democracy and then under fascist-military dictatorship, it is clear that both have failed. But the record of the military regime is clearly the most disgraceful.

The current SLORC leaders are but the "sons" of the godfather Ne Win. Socialist practices continue to be applied by dictatorial methods. Military capitalism reinforces the power of the elite to exploit the masses.

End Note

Aung San's seemingly contradictory confidences in Dorman-Smith, early in 1946 (refer to page 74), defy rational explanation. He appears to have said what he did instinctively, probably based on his awareness of the fate of national heroes in general, and those figuring in Burmese history in particular, wherein many had been betrayed and killed. His reference to "eighteen months" is inexplicable, but it is ironic that he was assassinated in mid-1947. On the other hand he was averse to ostentation and personal protection and felt secure in the affection of his people.

Appendix

Selected telegrams Concerning the Assassination and Trial

Sir Hubert Rance to Lord Pethick-Lawrence
Telegram, IOR: M/4/2504

MOST IMMEDIATE   RANGOON, *21 September 1946, 2300 hours*
                                 Received: 21 September, 2150 hours

No. 121 PERSONAL FROM GOVERNOR. An attempt was made on the life of U
Saw repeat U Saw, this afternoon not long after he had left Government House.
Saw's account, given to police officer, is that, after leaving Government House he
went to the Office of his paper [*the Sun*] and then crossed over to his headquarters
where he had short meeting. He left at about 16.30 hours to go home with two of
his party men following in car behind. When he reached the roundabout on the
Prome Road, in a quarter called Myenigon, about half mile from Government
House he looked round to see whether the other car was following. U Saw then
noted a jeep. When pulling up hill on the other side of the roundabout, he slowed
up for a bad stretch of the road. He looked round and noticed the jeep along side
with 4 PYT repeat PYT [*pyithu yebaw tathpwe*, i.e., the PVO], men in uniform and
muzzle of a weapon pointing at his car. One shot was fired which passed through
both windows. Jeep then drove away and Saw's car stopped. Saw was not hit by
bullet but has been badly cut about the eye by glass, apparently one eye being in
serious condition. He was taken to hospital by two Europeans passing by at the
time. Story is generally confirmed by Saw's secretary. Members of *Myochit* party
who set out with him and have since been interrogated, say this [is] beginning of
party war which police [have] been expecting. Saw had made a powerful challenge to AFPFL in his paper two days ago. Further investigations are being made.
I shall keep you informed.

2. CID report also that Saw's wife has been anxious to get rid of him on account of his so-called German wife in Uganda.

3. I saw Aung San, Paw Tun, Ba Maw, Saw and Ba Sein today. Aung San had to report to his Executive Council. I am seeing him again either tomorrow, Sunday afternoon, or Monday morning.[1]

4. Strike position not, repeat not, very hopeful. It has been a day of meetings and reports of meetings. I am seeing three non-official members of CLA Committee tomorrow, Sunday afternoon. They include Chairman of Joint Committee of Service Organisations.

Sir Hubert Rance to the Earl of Listowel
Telegram, IOR: M/4/2714

MOST IMMEDIATE   RANGOON, *19 July 1947, 1200 hours*
Received: 19 July, 0840 hours

No. 281. PERSONAL FROM GOVERNOR. An attack was made on Executive Council in Session at about 10.30 this morning by three Burmans armed with Sten guns. Casualties: killed—Razak, Ba Choe, Thakin Mya, Ba Win, Mahn Ba Khaing: Wounded—Aung San (wounded through chest), Möng Pawn *Sawbwa*. Full report will follow.[2]

R.W.D. Fowler (Acting Governor's Secretary) to Sir Gilbert Laithwaite
Telegram, IOR: M/4/2714

MOST IMMEDIATE   RANGOON, *19 July 1947, 1625 hours*
Received 19 July 1545 hours

No. 282. LAITHWAITE FROM FOWLER. Governor's personal telegram 281. I can now give you further details. At about 10.30 this morning when the Executive Council was in session a jeep with XIIth Army markings drew up to the main entrance. One man stayed in the jeep. Five men armed with Sten guns and two rifles went upstairs to the Council Chamber. An armed PVO on guard outside the door tried to stop them and was shot. He has identified the armed men as members of the 4th Burma Rifles. He was badly wounded and could not give any details.

The three men with Sten guns entered the Council Chamber and sprayed the occupants with bullets. They then made good their escape in the jeep.

2. The following casualties are now confirmed. Dead—Aung San, Ba Win, Abdul Razak, Mahn Ba Khaing, Thakin Mya and Ohn Maung, Deputy Secretary, Transport and Communications Department who was present at the Council Meeting. Wounded—Deedok Ba Choe (condition serious), the Sawbwa of Möng Pawn (condition good) and Ko Htwe, Personal Assistant to Abdul Razak.

3. Pyawbwe U Mya, U Ba Gyan, U Aung Zan Wai and Shwe Baw, Secretary to the Executive Council, are unhurt. Saw San Po Thin was on tour and Thakin Nu was of course not present at the meeting.

4. Casualties were sent to the general hospital without delay and the police seem to have dealt with the situation efficiently.

5. There are no indications at the moment to show whether this incident is part of a general insurrection or not. There are indications that the Red Flag Communists knew of the plan for this attack and there is also reason to believe that the other opposition parties feared that strong action was contemplated against them by the present Government. This suggests that all the Opposition parties may have been privy to the attack but there is of course no evidence of this.

6. His Excellency had discussions with General Briggs, General Thomas, the Inspector-General of Police, and others concerned with internal security this morning and Burma Command are taking precautions in case of further trouble.

7. His Excellency is at the moment in conference with Thakin Nu, U Aung Zan Wai, Pyawbwe U Mya and a further telegram will follow as soon as this Conference is completed with information about proposals for the formation of a new Council.

Sir Hubert Rance to the Earl of Listowel
Telegram, IOR: M/4/2714

MOST IMMEDIATE   RANGOON, *20 July 1947, 1015 hours*
                                   Received: 20 July, 0800 hours

No. 287. PERSONAL FROM GOVERNOR. My 281 and subsequent telegrams. Suspicion centres around U Saw. Shortly after 11 hours yesterday morning a jeep containing five men in singlets arrived at U Saw's residence. Yesterday afternoon the house was raided by the police and Saw and 10 men were taken into protective custody. 18 rifles and one Sten gun were found. Jeep in compound had no repeat no rear number plate and it is believed that jeep used by assailants in the morning also was without a rear plate.

Sir Hubert Rance to the Earl of Listowel
Telegram, IOR: M/4/2715

MOST IMMEDIATE   RANGOON, *21 July 1947, 1625 hours*
                                                      Received: 21 July, 1500 hours

No 294. PERSONAL FROM GOVERNOR. Certain sections of the Burmese press today adopted a definite anti-British trend. Rumours circulating are that British have given arms to opposition and sponsored attack on Council so that a Government can be formed favourable to HMG's policy of keeping Burma within the Empire. Reports are also circulating that I have given interviews to U Saw and Ba Maw in last ten days and asked them if they were prepared to form a Government if AFPFL fall. I have just seen Thakin Nu and emphasised complete falsity of rumours and emphasised also dangerous effects that may arise if today's press policy is allowed to continue. I have told Nu that he should summon a press conference today if possible and Government should also make a broadcast. Nu agreed.

2. The loss of the large number of Bren guns and ammunition is undoubtedly causing a great deal of excitement and it would seem that British officers are involved although there is as yet no definite proof. Nu wishes to set up a special tribunal to investigate the case and thinks that this will have a calming effect on the people. I am not sure of the legal aspects of such a tribunal in so far as the Army is concerned and would welcome your advice. I have sent McGuire to discuss with GOC.

Confidential Prime Minister's Room, RANGOON, *25 July, 1947*

It was decided: (a) that the following Press communique be immediately issued both in English and Burmese to dispel the doubt that both his Majesty's Government and His Excellency the Governor of Burma have something to do with the dastardly murders of the Hon'ble U Aung San and some of his colleagues; and (b) that all Commissioners and Deputy Commissioners be informed by telegram that the Government are using this Press Communique and that it be given as wide publicity as possible.

Press Communique

"Rumours connecting His Majesty's Government and His Excellency the Governor of Burma with the recent murders of the Hon'ble U Aung San and others of the Executive Council, have spread into certain sections of the public. The Government of Burma wish it to be known that these rumours are utterly unfounded and that there is closed understanding between His Majesty's Government His Excellency the Governor and the Burma Government. They are actively co-operating with the view to bringing the culprits to book, with the least possible delay."

Sir Hubert Rance to the Earl of Listowel
Telegram, IOR: M/4/2715

MOST IMMEDIATE   RANGOON, *28 July 1947, 1215 hrs*
SECRET   *Received: 28 July, 1430 hrs*

No.313. PERSONAL FROM GOVERNOR. Your 1689 26 July. I have attempted below to give a sequence of events with my comments and to show regretfully that if serious trouble arises in Burma the Army must accept a major share of responsibility.
    1. For some time past at weekly internal security meetings attended by the Defence Services, G of B, and civil police, allegations have been made by civil officials that leakage of arms was taking place from Army Depots, etc. The Defence authorities gave assurances that investigations would be started.
    2. On 15th. July Aung San and Pyawbwe U Mya, acting Home Member, saw me and told me that the previous night they had learnt that 200 Bren guns had been handed over some weeks previously by the Base Ordnance Depot(actual date 24th June) [to] persons unknown. Aung San was naturally very worried at this loss and also at the great time-lag between loss and discovery, as distribution of arms up-country had probably by now taken place. The Home Member told me that the

Government would have to work quickly and throw out a wide net. I understood from this remark that he intended to take into protective custody all Opposition leaders and their lieutenants pending investigation.

3. I saw the GOC the same day, and he informed [me] that the issue was made by the BOD in good faith. The civil police had received authority to draw 500 Brens and had been drawing from this allotment for some time. On 24th June a party purporting to be police had arrived at BOD with correct documents duly signed and 200 Brens, 800 spare barrels and a quantity of Bren magazines were issued .I have not yet seen results of Court of Inquiry but believe the actual number of Brens authorised for the police was 100 and not 500. In addition the Home Member told the GOC two or three days ago in my presence that he believed that former issues of Bren guns had not repeat not exceeded 10 in number, that verification of authority to issue was always obtained by telephone but not repeat not in this case, the number of police vehicles was always taken by BOD, not repeat not in this case, and police vehicles were easily distinguishable whereas the bogus police party used unmarked truck. I cannot repeat cannot confirm the accuracy of Home Member's remarks until I have seen Court of Inquiry.

4. GOC in course of conversation on 15th July said Major Moore, Commandant, the Base Ammunition Depot and connected with Base Ordnance Depot was suspect as result of investigations. It was believed that he was implicated in arms case in India during the war when he was a Warrant Officer in the IAOC. Further Moore was in Burma in prewar days as an NCO in IAOC and it was believed that he was then noted on the Civil Police Suspect List. The GOC then added that Moore had recently stated that U Saw when drunk had told him (Moore) that he had lots of arms buried in the lake. The GOC told me that he thought Moore had made this statement to deflect suspicion from himself as he knew that investigations into arms losses had started. The GOC also thought it improbable that U Saw would make such a disclosure. At this time I was unaware of the full contents of Moore's statement or that it was a written statement (see para 11 below). I was under the impression that it was purely a verbal remark.

5. On 16th July I saw Aung San and Thakin Nu in connection with the Goodwill Mission Declaration. In the course of the conversation when discussing the loss of the Brens I said to Aung San that there were rumours that U Saw was concealing arms in the lake and suggested that the lake be dragged.

6. On 18th July I visited Philip Nash in hospital and found that he knew of the loss of arms. Philip Nash gave me additional information that British officers

(afterwards discovered to be Hunt the DSO) had been watching Saw's bungalow at night with field glasses and had seen Saw with four or five men in a boat in somewhat suspicious circumstances on several occasions. Saw, however, was always well dressed and it was presumed by the watcher that it was the case of a woman.

7. Later the same day I saw Thakin Nu again in connection with Goodwill Mission Declaration. I urged Nu again to get the lake by U Saw's house dragged and told him of the report of the night watcher. Nu then told me of the great loss of ammunition which had occurred on the 12th July at the Base Ammunition Depot north of Mingaladon and many miles from the BOD. Apparently the same procedure adopted for the BOD had been used and the ruse was again successful. The disquieting news from Nu however was that Saw visited the Depot one hour after the theft and was believed to have had tea in the Depot. The theft was confirmed to me later on 18th July by Brigadier Nash.

8. The 19th July was the day of the assassination. At one of many meetings I held on that fateful day the IGP told me that plan had been made for some 200 people to be taken into protective custody the following day Sunday 20th July. It may be that the assassination was always destined for 19th July when it would be well known that there was an Executive Council meeting or it may have been that the news of the proposed round-up leaked out and forced the instigators to take immediate action.

9. It is difficult to appreciate what was in the minds of the instigators. My own view is that the plan of certain elements of the Opposition was to collect arms by stealth and gradually to prepare the way for armed civil strife and a fight for power. It may well be that emboldened by their success in obtaining arms in small quantities without apparent detection the loss of a large quantity (but small in comparison with the holdings of the BOD and BAD) might also well escape detection especially if there were friends among the Depot's officers. I cannot believe that the Opposition would attempt a 'coup d' etat' at this time when Imperial troops in the country still constitute a considerable force. The logical plan would be to await a more favourable time a few months later when troops had left. It may be, however, that this seems fantastic that the Opposition expected Military Government to be reinstituted as the result of a successful assassination of AFPFL leaders and that in time the loss would result in major divisions within AFPFL. One must not overlook the possibility of the authors planned assassination first of personal enemies as a prelude to a state of anarchy without a clear-thought out plan of the future.

10. At weekly Internal Security meeting Tuesday 22nd July it was reported to me that there was a certain amount of feeling between Civil and Defence Services representatives: the civil authorities complaining of lack of knowledge of measures taken by army resulting from thefts and assassination(sic). I accordingly arranged a meeting in my office the following day between GOC, BGS, Home Member, and Defence Counsellor and a daily visit by a liaison officer from army to Government was arranged.

11. Since the assassinations, fear has been widespread and anti-British agitation had arisen based on the knowledge of the major thefts from the Depots and assisted by rumour and conjecture. For a few days this agitation undoubtedly existed, but in the past two or three days the tension definitely eased due to action by Nu and others. On the morning of 25th July the GOC and Brigadier Duke the BGS visited me and showed me a copy of Moore's statement (para 3 above) made originally to one investigating officer on 26th June and repeated in writing to the DPM Burma Command on 5th July. This statement repeated to you in succeeding telegram had not repeat not been shown to CID through an oversight over the part of Duke. The statement was obtained when GOC and BGS (Duke) were in Singapore for F.M. Montgomery's visit, and Duke on return after showing to the GOC put the document away. The discovery later of the thefts firstly at BOD and later at BAD did not remind Duke of the document and vital importance of its contents - it was only after the assassination that Duke remembered and then decided to report the matter as soon as the tension abated. Duke has been very open over the whole affair and accepts all blame. In extenuation it can be said that he first saw Moore's statement on 8th July and doubtless imagined that action had already been taken and civil authorities informed but unfortunately did not verify that this was so.

12. The existence of Moore's statement is almost certain to come to light in CID investigations and if the news becomes public it is certain to arouse anti-British feelings to a pitch that may well become most serious. Yesterday evening I summoned Thakin Nu, Pyawbwe U Mya, GOC and BGS and the unfortunate story was retold. The Burmese Ministers took it very well and acknowledged the danger if the news became public, with a possible clarion call by the Press that the assassination could have been averted. They appreciated also too well how difficult it will be to prevent a leakage, but promised all help.

13. In view of the above events I would sooner that a more facile pen than mine drafted the Prime Minister's answer. The Government are releasing little information regarding crime, although I understand that they have established beyond doubt that the author of the thefts and assassination was the same person

i.e. presumably Saw. They are now trying to find connections between the author and other parties and so unearth the whole plot. The Prime Minister can quote the incident of thefts, as it is common knowledge here; although it may be advisable to say large quantities of arms and ammunition rather than quoting figures. No repeat no reference should be made to Moore. Courts of Inquiry were started by the army immediately but will take time as some of the witnesses are not readily available. There is no doubt that this was a plot to throw the country into a state of anarchy either now or in the immediate future.

14. I will keep you informed of further developments. I agree with Dryden "Ill fortune seldom comes alone".[3]

This was followed by another telegram, despatched 1725 hours:
No. 319

PERSONAL FROM GOVERNOR. Para No. 3 of my telegram 313 28th July. Exact figures for arms removed from BOD have now been verified and are as follows:
(a) Bren 200 each complete with 1 spare barrel;
(b) 200 additional spare barrels;
(c) 800 Bren magazines.
These arms were removed from the BOD on 24th June.
Removal of ammunition from ARD took place on 12th July.

Sir Hubert Rance to the Earl of Listowel
Telegram, IOR: M/4/2715

MOST IMMEDIATE   RANGOON, *28 July 1947, 1255 hrs*
TOP SECRET   *Received:28 July, 1723 hrs*

No. 314. PERSONAL FROM GOVERNOR. My immediately preceding telegram. Here is the text of Moore's statement to Burma Command.
Begins.
2. Reference No. M/47 Ammunition Depot (Burma) Mingaladon P.O. 5/7/47 to DPM, HQ Burma Command. Subject security. Reference—conversation Lt.Col Dobson—Major Moore.

3. Early in June this year I became acquainted with Captain (now Major) Daine of "X" Branch HQ Burma Command. I invited him to luncheon to discuss mutual interest in ballistics.

4. After luncheon the conversation veered to Burma's personalities and Daine asked me if I would care to meet U Saw. I replied that I would, and a few evenings later Daine and U Saw kept the appointment and were introduced to Capt Shenoi and Lt Hujsey of the Ammunition Depot and F/Lts Edwards and Britten of the RAF Explosives Section.

5. After an hour or so Daine and U Saw left but before leaving U Saw extended an open invitation to all the officers "to drop into his place at any time for a drink" and a further invitation to my wife and I to come to luncheon on the following Saturday to "meet Mrs U Saw".

6. I kept the luncheon appointment with my eleven-year-old daughter, my wife being indisposed. Daine was at the luncheon. Shortly after luncheon I left to keep a football appointment in Rangoon but was invited to return after the football match for a drink.

7. I returned at about dusk and consequent on my remarking on (a) the number of armed personnel at the gate and around the bungalow and (b) the arms, small arms ammunition, and hand grenades in U Saw's bedroom the following statements were made in the course of a long conversation by U Saw (i) the armed sentries, and arms, etc. in his bedroom were essential to his well being: (ii) that his source of supply was from local units in small quantities at any one time: (iii) that he was expecting delivery in the very near future of 5 lorry loads of arms from an individual he thought was an officer. These were to be delivered when the individual's Major returned from hospital or sick leave: (iv) that he was expecting a large number of revolvers from an Anglo-Burman Excise Official, resident in Insein: (v) that he required more arms and ammunition, storage of which would be effected as had been done in the past by placing them in airtight containers and sinking the containers in Victoria Lake in various spots at least two furlongs distance from his bungalow and marking the spots by taking visual bearing on any two visual objects.

8. The conversation was interrupted by the arrival of Mr Malhotra of Leele and Co, resident at Fytche Road Rangoon after which I came home but before my departure extended an invitation to U Saw to bring Mrs U Saw to tea two or three days later. This appointment was kept but only general conversation took place.

9. One evening in about the second week of June whilst returning from Rangoon together with F/Lts Edwards and Britten we accepted U Saw's general

invitation to drop in for a drink. Edwards remarking on the close scrutiny by the guards at the gate, opened the conversation on arms and ammunition once more and in the course of a long conversation during which several drinks were consumed the following statements were made by U Saw, both of his own accord and in reply to questions—(i) that the promises of three lorry loads of arms and the arms from Insein had not materialised: (ii) that the dealings with the individuals who had promised the three lorry loads, had been done on a small scale for some months, and that he thought that the individual was an officer from the BOD: (iii) that his holdings of cartridges, SA ball, .455 inch revolver Mk 6 jacketed ammunition of which we were shown samples had come from that source. (It was pointed out to U Saw that this ammunition was not equipment in Burma and had not been held by ORD since the reoccupation of Burma but he reiterated his statement that he obtained [it] from that source): (iv) that the usual procedure was for his jeep to go and collect from appointed places but that on one or two occasions ammunition had been brought to him in containers such as petrol tins which were immediately sealed and placed in the lake.

10. This conversation was interrupted by the arrival of Daine who was dressed in a light blue longyi, a white shirt and gold embroidered "chapplie" accompanied by Mr Malhotra. The former came into the house while the latter remained outside in a jeep. They did not stay long and immediately after their departure at U Saw's invitation we accompanied him to Nam Sing restaurant where we were his guests to a Chinese dinner after which we returned to our respective residences.

11. I am unable to substantiate these statements inasmuch that the first set of remarks were made to me alone, and no other person was present. The second set of statements were made whilst Edwards and Britten were in the room but I am unable to state exactly how much of the conversation they heard. A statement from Edwards is invited. Britten having proceeded ex Burma.

12. Realising that I was in possession of information that had a direct bearing on security, which information I was not in a position to substantiate, I volunteered the information to the Brigade Intelligence Officer, Capt. Smart, stressing the point that I could neither substantiate nor give the information on oath. (Signed Major J.A. Moore) Major IAOC, OC Ammunition Depot (Burma)[4] Ends.

Sir Hubert Rance to the Earl of Listowel
Telegram, IOR: M/4/2714

Appendix

IMPORTANT   RANGOON, *28 July 1947, 1725 hours*
                                           Received 28 July, 2100 hours

No. 318. PERSONAL FROM GOVERNOR

1. I saw Tin Tut and Kyaw Nyein this morning. The latter as a result of his visit to Yugoslavia is convinced that the country is a closely controlled Communist state and is run on Soviet lines. In his opinion there was no question of it being a democratic form of state, in the accepted sense of the word democracy.

2. The conversation naturally turned to the recent tragic events here. Kyaw Nyein horrified me by telling me that U Saw must have been subsidised, and that in his opinion European business firms had probably helped U Saw. I told Kyaw Nyein that I was both surprised and dismayed that a person holding such a responsible position as Home Member should make such an accusation. I added that I had been horrified at the assassination but that I would even be more horrified if such an accusation were proved. In this connection I quote an extract from the 'Guide Daily' of 28th July: "Last January when the Delegation headed by U Aung San signed the Aung San-Attlee Agreement U Saw and Thakin Ba Sein refused to sign and U Saw remained behind when all others had returned. We (The Guide Daily) had already told the country that U Saw remained purposely behind to plan for the destruction of AFPFL with the help of the white man who at the time had given 5 lakhs to him (Saw).

3. We have again come to know that while U Saw was in England it was some of the English Capitalists who aided him with lots of money. It will be very interesting when the trial begins as all these secrets will be exposed."

4. My telegram 313 of today's date is also pertinent. We are certainly not repeat not out of the wood yet in so far as blame for the crime is concerned.

Sir Hubert Rance to the Earl of Listowel
Telegram, IOR: M/4/2714

IMPORTANT   RANGOON, *28th. July, 1835 hours*
SECRET   *Received: 28 July, 2100 hours*

No. 320. PERSONAL FROM GOVERNOR. Following cable has been received by me from Maung Jee or Gyee, 132 Great Portland Street, London W1.

Begins. My cables for unknown reasons have not reached U Saw's family or his friends. As his brother, I shall be most grateful if your Excellency will convey this message to him. Message reads: Your friends in Parliament advise me arrange at this end preparations for your defence in view of serious repercussions likely to arise out of the present situation. Concurring with this view and being much worried for your safety I implore you to instruct Bank to remit by cable three hundred pounds urgently required for immediate preparations, obtaining King's Counsel and for work likely to be useful in your defence. Send your instructions to the Bank and your reply to me through kind favour His Excellency. Message Ends. May I crave your Excellency's indulgence not to divulge this cable to Burmese members of Government. Ends.

I have transmitted the text of the message only repeat only to Honourable Home Minister for conveyance through appropriate channels to U Saw. Obviously I could not accept Maung Jee's request last para.

I notice in recent ISS report from South Burma Area that this same Maung Jee has sent a cable addressed to Han Tin stating that if Han Tin was unable to obtain £300 from Saw's wife he is advised to approach directors of Sun Press. He said he required this money for preliminary arrangements in connection with Saw's defence. Han Tin is in custody.

I am sending by mail copy of interesting letter written to U Saw from Maung Jee on 17th July 1946.

No. 321. PERSONAL FROM GOVERNOR
29th July, 1250 hours

Total Brens recovered to date now 149, namely 80 from U Saw's house and Rangoon area, 12 from Prome and 57 from Tharawaddy. These figures not public. But I suggest that Prime Minister could say that of the arms that were removed through a clever forgery from an army depot in Rangoon recent reports indicate that a majority of these have been recovered. Meanwhile investigations by the police, with the cooperation of the military authorities, are still being vigorously pushed in relation to these thefts.

Situation is still quiet and nothing unusual to report.

Government is considering whether to elaborate further communiques by indicating more fully results of investigations into murders. My telegram 315 28/7 refers. I have asked Thakin Nu whether this could be done quickly so that if there is anything further to say I could send it to you in time for Prime Minister's statement.

U Saw to Sir Hubert Rance
IOR: M/4/2721   INSEIN CENTRAL JAIL *29th July 1947*

It appears to me that the Officers of the Police Dept. of Govt. of Burma have, under the strong pressure of the Party in Power, been concentrating the whole of their time and energy on placing us, the members of the Opposition, by all means before a Court for trial in connection with the Shooting Case that has recently occurred in the Secretariat Building, Rangoon.

I apprehend that the police have been employing the usual method of forcing some persons arrested to say what they wanted them to say by means of torturing them in one or more different ways . My apprehension is, I submit, not groundless for I have the strong feeling that [a] few days after we were brought into the Jail, some Police Officers came in and started examining some of the persons arrested and that after having examined some of them they did not continue to examine the rest. What I have been anxiously afraid is that those persons would have been taken out of the Jail and forced to make such statements as the Police desire.

To have a Case tried by an impartial Court or Tribunal sounds very grand but at the same time the Court or Tribunal has to go according to the evidence produced by the Police . There were many cases in the past where the Court had no alternative but to accept the evidence produced by the Police although the Judge or Judges knew perfectly well that the evidence so produced was as false as it was fabricated or concocted by the Police. The point I am trying to submit to your Excellency is that the present stage at which the Police officers obviously, under direct pressure of the Member or Members of the Party in Power, trying to smash us by all possible means, is an early but very important stage.

My humble request to your Excellency, therefore is to approach His Majesty's Government to send out Special Police Officers to this Country for the purpose of investigating into the Case.

I hope and trust your Excellency will be good enough to forward this humble request of mine to his Majesty's Government with your recommendation if possible in the interest of justice and fair play.[5]

Council of Ministers, 1st. Special Meeting, Minute IOR:M/4/2555

Present: Thakin Nu (in the Chair), U Mya (Pyawbwe), U Aung Zan Wai, U Ba Gyan, Thakin Lun Baw, U Mya (Henzada), Thakin Tin, Bo Let Ya, U Win, Bo Po Kun, U Pe Kin.

#337 Sir Hubert Rance to the Earl of Listowel

RANGOON, *2 August, 1947, 1145 hours*

2(b) Saw told his followers that it was certain that when the leaders of AFPFL were removed HE would send for Saw and ask him to form a Government. This sounds incredible and all I can suggest, if this information is true, is that Saw anticipated that suspicion for the crime would fall on one or other of the Communist parties.

South East Asia Land Forces to War Office
Telegram, IOR: L/WS/1/669

IMMEDIATE   SINGAPORE, *6 August, 1947, 1230 hours*

12804/Intelligence: Burma resume till 3 August.

1 Moderation gaining ground and situation quiet. Must however consider following possibilities:
   a   Anti-British outbreak.
   b   Attempts by BCP to undermine government.
   c   Attempts by opposition parties to overthrow government.
   d   BCP-AFPFL coalition.
Danger of (a) lessening but anti-British propaganda continues and any untoward incident might again produce grave tension and danger. Example of such incidents might be popular belief British complicity in murders, or widespread suspicion of British good faith or inter-racial incident, (b) seems likely, (c) at present discounted but consider should not be excluded, (d) seems unlikely

because BCP would open mouths too wide. It appears most likely that AFPFL will be left to hold the Government together until independence is achieved but with growing opposition.

2. Burma Army. Possible that with perhaps the exception of few Gurkha elements the Army will remain loyal to and support the Burma Government. Chins, Kachins and Karens might however be lukewarm due to politically disinterested outlook. It may be assumed that the Burma Army feels no loyalty to British interests, or obligations to support them. These broad generalisations on possible attitude Burma Army indicate that it would probably be a stabilising factor in cases (b) (c) (d). In case (a) its value as a stabilising factor would depend on the degree in which the existing government shared or resisted, and wished to restrain anti-British feeling.

3. Conclusion. Although Thakin Nu is superior as a statesman to Aung San he lacks the popular appeal and coupled with public apathy towards the newly-elected ministry the result is a government open to opposition broadsides.

4. Above moves trends and possibilities as at present seen by GSI Singapore.

It is of interest to note that prior to the dispatch of the above communication Sir Hubert had advised the Earl of Listowel, in a personal message dated 30 July, that he had had a talk with Ralph Stoneham that morning, described by him "as one of the most popular Europeans in this country" who had told him of a noticeable change in the feelings to him of Burmese friends since the assassination.

General Sir Neil Ritchie to Field Marshall Montgomery
Telegram IOR: M/4/2715

MOST IMMEDIAT   SINGAPORE, *7 August, 2147 hours*
TOP SECRET

1011/MA Jakin. PERSONAL FOR CIGS FROM RITCHIE. Subject is further details respecting Burma.
(Only paras. 3, 4, and 5 are quoted below:)

3. I informed Governor in conversation on 15 July that Moore had made this statement and gave Governor gist of it, presuming that investigations were going on in civil as well as in military channels. Governor mentioned to Aung San and

Thakin Nu that he had heard that U Saw was hiding arms in the lake near his house.

4. Understanding Aung San was informed by CID of plot against ministers for 20 July, and in consequence was actually discussing with ministers large scale arrests including U Saw at moment of assassinations. It is important to note that arms used for assassinations were a type different to those obtained from AOU [sic: AOD?]

5. Correct date of assassination was 19 July. I think we got this wrong from Greenwood but cannot check as I [Ritchie] am on tour and have no copy of your signal with me.

Sir Reginald Dorman-Smith to the Earl of Listowel
IOR: L/PO/9/7

PRIVATE AND CONFIDENTIAL
STODHAM PARK, LISS, HAMPSHIRE   *10 August 1947*

I see that U Saw is to stand his trial for the assassination of Aung San and his AFPFL colleagues. I have, of course, no idea what evidence there is against Saw or whether he is innocent or guilty of this foul crime. I can, however, visualise the possibility that, in fighting for his life, Saw may wish to cover quite a lot of past history to show, for example, that he has always been a good Burmese patriot and, in contrast to Aung San and AFPFL, a good democrat. It is just conceivable that he might wish to summon me as one of his witnesses.

It probably would be more than a little embarrassing both for me myself and for HMG if I were to take any part in this trial but, in spite of this, I feel that I should try to help if called upon. It is not that I have any illusions about Saw whom I know too well for that! I did, however, always find him a good personal friend and a wise adviser. However badly he may have tripped up after leaving Burma in 1941, he was of the greatest help to me in my efforts to get Burma into some kind of shape to meet an invasion. I would hate him to think that I would be unwilling to speak for him now in his hour of greatest need.

Aung San's assassination puzzles me a lot. When I last met Saw and U Ba Yin they were very outspoken about the "Fascist" tendencies of AFPFL and the need for developing a proper democratic outlook for Burma. Saw was a frightened man, convinced that it was AFPFL who tried to murder him in his motor car but they spoke hotly against the use of assassination as a means to gain political ends. Saw is an ambitious man and I know that it was rumoured in pre-war days that one or two of his opponents had died a bit suddenly but to organise and execute a blood-bath seems to me to be out of keeping with Saw's character.

I should be glad to know whether you agree with me that it would be my duty to give evidence if called upon to do so.

Sir Hubert Rance to the Earl of Listowel
Telegram, IOR: M/4/2714

MOST IMMEDIATE   RANGOON, *25 August 1947, 1015 hours*
SECRET   *Received: 25 August, 1050 hours*

NO. 408. PERSONAL FROM GOVERNOR. On Saturday 23 August at 9.00pm Kyaw Nyein, Home Minister, came urgently to see me and produced copies of two letters written by U Saw in Insein Jail and handed over to authorities by jailer who though bribed by Saw to take his correspondence is showing it (presumably unknown to Saw) to authorities.

2. These letters were dated 22nd and 23rd and were addressed to Bingley of the British Council. They asked for his aid and used curious phrases which might mean some form of identifying code. They referred to one "(VV)" who must be Vivian. They talked not only of hopes of escape but also of threats to make disclosures which would have both internal and international repercussions. They assured Bingley that the messenger bringing them could be trusted.

3. Bingley did not receive these letters. The messenger was allowed to bring one of them, but on arrival at the house was brushed aside by Bingley who was just about to leave for BOAC hostel to stay the night before leaving for UK next morning.

4. In the opinion of the Police these letters connect Bingley with the "tall gentleman" to whom reference has been made in other letters written from jail by Saw, including one to Vivian.

5. As you can imagine all this was most disturbing. I can hardly credit Bingley with intriguing, but however innocent on his side his dealings with Saw may have been it is obvious that in the light of these letters the worst interpretation could be put on them.

6. There was clearly only one course for me to take and that was to stop Bingley from leaving and to get him questioned. Accordingly at that late hour I

had Bingley contacted at BOAC hostel and asked him not to leave and I requested BOAC to defer his passage.

7. Yesterday, Sunday, McGuire took Tun Hla Oung, DIG CID, to Bingley's house and left him there to question Bingley.

8. McGuire informs me that when he went to see Tun Hla Oung yesterday evening he found him with Kyaw Nyein discussing the case. He was told that Bingley had been questioned for five hours and that the result was not repeat not satisfactory though Tun Hla Oung mentioned that proof was difficult and that he did not think Bingley had been trying to get letters to Saw.

9. Kyaw Nyein also told McGuire that he would now have to place the whole matter before the cabinet. He said that he would do this today and would try to come with Thakin Nu to see me this evening.

10. At the moment all this has been kept within the knowledge of the fewest possible persons. But naturally I am gravely concerned as to what may leak out and to the misinterpretations that might be made.

11. I am seeing Bingley this morning. I hope that after this evening's talk with Kyaw Nyein and Thakin Nu I shall have more details to enable me to assess this affair more clearly.

12. Jenkins who is Bingley's successor is sending a guarded cable to British Council.

Sir Hubert Rance to the Earl of Listowel
Telegram, IOR: M/4/2714

MOST IMMEDIATE   RANGOON, *27 August 1947, 0930 hours*
SECRET   *Received: 27 August, 0045 hours*

No 419. PERSONAL FROM GOVERNOR. My telegrams 408, 410 and 412. Bingley. I saw Thakin Nu and Kyaw Nyein this morning and we discussed amongst other matters the case of Bingley.

2. There is no doubt that the Ministers are intensely suspicious of Bingley and it would seem necessary that Bingley should stay here until suspicion is cleared. Points disclosed today by Kyaw Nyein and not reported in my previous telegrams are as follows.

3. Chief jailer in Saw's jail although heavily bribed by Saw is reporting all information obtained and handing all messages written by Saw to outside friends to Governor [of the jail].

4. Saw in his early days in jail communicated to other co-accused in same jail that they were not to worry as he had three ex-Governors and many ex-Ministers in England on his side. Later he mentioned a tall friend in Burma who possessed great influence and who would see that no harm came to them. Saw also mentioned this tall friend to Vivian in one of his letters and Vivian is reported in his reply to have advised Saw not repeat not to bring the tall friend into the affair at present.

5. As the days passed Saw became worried and wrote to another friend outside asking his advice regarding the tall friend. The Government, perturbed about the identity of the tall friend, now took a hand. A letter purporting to come from Saw's friend was handed to Saw advising him to contact the tall friend immediately. The ruse was successful and Saw wrote two letters to Bingley referred to in my telegram 408, 25 August.

6. A passage in Saw's second letter to Bingley and which is causing grave suspicion in the minds of the Ministers reads: "I took a grave risk as advised."

7. Other points brought out in my conversation with the two Ministers were:

(a) Nu believes that the British Council is a cloak for some intelligence organisation. I did my best to dispel this idea but until the Bingley affair is cleared the suspicion will I think remain.

(b) Nu was suspicious of Bingley's apparent sudden departure from Burma. Here I was able to produce a letter from Laithwaite sent to me in July which stated that Bingley was required to be in England in September for a meeting of the British Council.

(c) Kyaw Nyein said that when Saw mentioned his tall friend to the chief jailer, the latter said: "I hope it isn't the Governor." To this Saw replied that the Governor was no use as he had already been bought by Aung San and Thakin Nu for twelve lakhs [1,200,000].

8. I still think Bingley is a victim of circumstances but time will show.

General Sir Neil Ritchie to Sir Henry MacGeagh
Telegram, IOR: M/4/2715

MOST IMMEDIATE   SINGAPORE, *29 August 1947, 1920 hours*
TOP SECRET

No. 18927/AG3. Personal for JAG from Ritchie. Further to my 18778 AG3 of 25 August and my 18927 AG3 of 29 August, in order to keep you in the picture I have summarised the situation as far as I know it with regard to the theft of arms from 226 AOD Burma and AAD[6] Burma and also the Civil Investigations into the recent assassinations.

1. Brit Military court of enquiry into the theft of arms and ammunition are now complete and are being forwarded to you by hand of officer (see this GHQ Signal 18802 AG3 of 26 August). An account of the results of these inquiries was given in my 10511 AG3 of 25 August.

2. With regard to the civil enquiries into the assassination the following officers appear to be implicated.

(a) Capt Vivian, Indian Army, seconded to the Rangoon Police, has been arrested by the civil police and almost certainly implicated with U Saw and also probably had a good deal to do with the thefts of arms and ammunition.

(b) Major Young IEME has been arrested by the civil police [on 24 August] and is suspected of selling weapons to U Saw see my 18926 AG3 of 29 August which gives the details.

(c) Major Moore OC, AAD, who was in hospital at the time of the thefts of ammunition, is known to have been an acquaintance of U Saw and also to have received U Saw in his house on at least one occasion. Civil police are investigating his case but so far no report of his arrest has reached me.

(d) Major Daine, Cipher Officer, HQ Burma Command: this officer is also under suspicion as he was an amateur collector of arms, and had an unusual quantity in his possession, he is also suspected of being a possible link between U Saw and Moore. He is not under arrest.

3. The cases of all the above are being investigated by the civil police and so far information has been scarce, but will keep you informed of any further information given to the military by the civil.

References

Aung San. *Burma's Challenge*. Rangoon: Tathetta Sarpay Taik, 1968.

Aung San Suu Kyi. *Burma and India: Some Aspects of Intellectual Life under Colonialism*. New Delhi: Indian Institute of Advanced Study & Allied Publishers, 1990.

——————. *Aung San of Burma*. Edinburgh: Kiscadale, 1991.

——————. *Freedom from Fear*. London: Penguin Books, 1991.

Aung Saw Oo. *Reflections on Aung San Suu Kyi*, Chiang Mai, Thailand, 1991.

Cady, John F. *A History of Modern Burma*. Ithaca and London: Cornell University Press, Fifth printing 1978.

Collis, Maurice. *Last and First in Burma (1941–1948)*. London: Faber & Faber, 1956.

Htin Aung. *History of Burma: From the Earliest Times to 10 March 1824, the Beginning of the English Conquest*. London: Longmans, Green, 1925.

Izumiya, Tatsuro. *The Minami Organ*. Rangoon: Arts and Science University, 1985.

Kyaw Min. *The Burma We Love*. Calcutta: India Book House, 1945.

Kyin Ho, Dr. *Bogyoke Aung San hne Myanma Arzanimya Lokkyan Hmugyi Atwinyemya* ("The Inside Story of the Assassination of General Aung San and Burma's Martyrs"). Fort Lauderdale, Florida: 1992.

Lintner, Bertil. *Outrage: Burma's Struggle for Democracy*. London: White Lotus UK, 1990.

——————. *Aung San Suu Kyi and Burma's Unfinished Renaissance*. Bangkok: White Lotus, 1991.

Maung Maung, ex-Brigadier. *From Sangha to Laity: Nationalist Movements of Burma 1920–1940*. New Delhi: Manohar (for the Australian National University), 1980.

——————. *Burmese Nationalist Movements 1940–1948*. Edinburgh: Kiscadale, 1989.

Maung Maung, Dr. *A Trial in Burma: the Assassination of Aung San*. The Hague: Martinus Nijhoff, 1962.

References

_____. *Burma and General Ne Win*. Bombay: Asia Publishing House, 1969.

_____. *Burma's Constitution*, The Hague, Martinus Nijhoff, 1959,

_____. (ed). *Aung San of Burma*. The Hague: Martinus Nijhoff (for Yale University Southeast Asia Studies), 1962.

Maung Maung Gyi. *Burmese Political Values: the Socio-Political Roots of Authoritarianism*. New York: Praeger, 1983.

Maung Maung Pye. *Burma in the Crucible*. Rangoon: Khittaya Publishing House, 1952.

Mya Sein, Daw. *The Administration of Burma*. Kuala Lumpur; Singapore; London: Oxford University Press, 1973.

Nu, U. *Saturday's Son: Memoirs of the Former Prime Minister of Burma*. Bombay: Bharatiya Vidya Bhavan, 1976.

Pye, Lucian W. *Politics, Personality and Nation Building: Burma's Search for Identity*. New Haven, Connecticut: Yale University Press, 1962.

Silverstein, Josef. *The Political Legacy of Aung San*. Ithaca: Southeast Asia Programme Data Paper No. 86, 1972.

_____. *Burma: Military Rule and the Politics of Stagnation*. Ithaca and London: Cornell University Press, 1977.

Tinker, Hugh. *The Union of Burma: A Study of The First Years of Independence*. London: Oxford University Press, 1957.

_____. *Burma: The Struggle for Independence 1944–1948* (in two volumes). London: Her Majesty's Stationery Office, 1984.

Trager, Frank N. *Burma: From Kingdom to Republic*. London: Pall Mall Press, 1966.

Tzang Yawnghwe, Chao. *The Shan of Burma: Memoirs of a Shan Exile*. Singapore: Institute of Southeast Asian Studies, 1987.

Ziegler, Phillip. *Mountbatten*, Perrenial Library, Harper & Row, 1985.

Books in Burmese

Bohmu Ba Thaung (Maung Thu Ta). *Bama Tawhlan-ye Thamaing*, Rangoon, 1972.

Khin Maung Nyo. *A Nya-ta-ra Sit-thi Ta U i Hmat-tan, Rangoon, 1969*.

Kyemon U Thaung. *Bo Ne Win i Sit-damya Lanzin*, Manerplaw, 1994.

Maung Pyithu. *Si Ar Di Bi tho ma-hoke Pye-pyay Tit-kyaw-pyan*, Ministry of Information, Rangoon, 1990.

Mya Daung Nyo. *Yebaw Thone Gyaik*, Rangoon, 1993.

Shwe Ka Laung. *Khit-a-laik Thadinsa Myar ko Lai-lar thone-thut Kye ya Wai*, 1st Impression, Ministry of Information, Rangoon 1992.

Government Publications in English

Is Trust Vindicated, the Chronicle of a Trust, Striving and Triumph, Director of Information, Government of the Union of Burma, 1960.

The Conspiracy of Treasonous Minions within the Myanmar Naing-gan and Traitorous Cohorts Abroad, Ministry of Information, Government of Myanmar, Rangoon, 1989.

Notes

Dramatis Personae

[1] The names in the lists of martyrs, assassins, and the law are arranged in order of seniority, rank, and importance in the Burmese way.

1
The General Has Been Shot

[1] Aung San Lin died at the age of 7, when he drowned in a muddy pond in the garden of their home in Tower Lane in Rangoon.

2
The Martyrs

[1] Later known as Bo Yan Aung, he joined the Communist insurrection in 1948.
[2] When Burma was declared an Independent State on 1 August 1943, the Tricolour flag, with a stylized peacock in the centre, was adopted as the national flag.

4
The Mystery

[1] No currency was specified, but presumably the paper meant rupees.
[2] Quotations are extracts from the Judgment of the Special Tribunal, Rangoon, sitting at Insein. Trial #1 of 1947.

5
Unanswered Questions

[1] See Appendix: Selected Telegrams from the Colonial Authorities in Rangoon to London.
[2] Released on 10 July 1995 after almost six years of house arrest.

Notes

3 See Appendix: Telegram IOR:M/4/2714. 19 July 1947.
4 Ne Win was an avid gambler and a frequent visitor to the Rangoon Race Course.

6
A Legacy of Violence

1 No relation to army chief Gen. Tin U who was ousted in 1976.

7
Postscript

1 Thakin Nu's broadcast - 22 July,1947
2 Edited and published by Dr U Kyaw Win, Orange Coast College, California, USA.
3 Hugh Tinker's *Burma: The Struggle for Independence 1944-48,* p 872.
4 Sir Ba U was at the time Judge of the High Court,and an important member of the Constitution Committee. He became the nation's President 1952-57.
5 Oliver Goldsmith's "The Good-Natured Man".

Appendix
Selected telegrams Concerning the Assassination and Trial

1 Next day, Rance informed Pethick-Lawrence in a Personal telegram No 122, 2015 hours, that he had again met Aung San to discuss names for the new Executive Council: he added "Conversation was friendly". He also reported meeting strike leaders who eventually agreed to reopen negotiations. There was nothing to indicate that Aung San had been behind any attempt on U Saw's life.
2 This telegram was apparently sent in a haste as soon as the Governor learnt about the assassination—Aung San died on the spot.
3 John Dryden, Epistles: To Mr Congreve
4 Rance further informed Listowel in telegram No. 372, 14 August, 1947, 1550 hours: Moore's statement has not repeat not been publicised and I hope will remain Top Secret.
5 Rance handed this letter to the Home Minister who noted: There is no need to make a reply.
6 AOD and AAD: the Base Ordnance Depot and Base Ammunition Depot in Rangoon.

Glossary

AFPFL. The Anti-Fascist People's Freedom League. Set up by Aung San and other nationalist leaders at the end of World War Two to fight the Japanese and became independent Burma's most powerful political institution. It split in 1958 into two factions, a "Clean" AFPFL led by Kyaw Nyein and Ba Swe and a "Stable" AFPFL led by U Nu. U Nu's faction was renamed the *Pyidaungsu* ("Union") Party before the 1960 election.

Arzani. "Martyr". 19 July is commemorated in Burma as *Arzani* Day.

BIA. The Burma Independence Army. Founded by Aung San in Bangkok, Thailand, on 26 December 1941, to fight for Burma's independence from Britain. Became the Burma Defence Army (BDA) in July 1942, the Burma National Army (BNA) in August 1943, and the Patriotic Burmese Forces (PBF) towards the end of the war. First allied with the Japanese but turned against them on 27 March 1945.

Bogyoke. "General". *Bogyokegyi* "Great General".

BSPP. The Burma Socialist Programme Party. Set up by Gen. Ne Win shortly after his *coup d'état* in March 1962. Burma's only legally permitted organisation until 1988. Now renamed the National Unity Party (NUP).

CPB. The Communist Party of Burma. Formed on 15 August 1939 in Rangoon. Led by Thakin Than Tun who led it underground shortly after Burma's independence in early 1948. In armed insurrection until 1989 when it collapsed following a mutiny among its rank and file.

Dacoit. An Anglo-Indian term meaning member of an armed band (from Hindi *dakait*, gang-robber).

Dohbama Asiayone. "Our Burma Association", or "We Burmans League". The most intensely nationalistic movement in Burma prior to World War Two. Almost all Burmese nationalist leaders were at one stage members of the organisation: Aung San, U Nu, Kyaw Nyein, U Razak, Ne Win, Thakin Than Tun, and many others.

Durbar. Court of Indian ruler (Urdu, from Persian: *darbar*, court). Later used for public levee of Indian prince or British governor or viceroy.

Galon. In Sanskrit: "Garuda". A powerful bird in Hindu mythology. In Burma the followers of Saya San (leader of a peasant rebellion in the 1930s) called themselves *galons*; later the term was used by U Saw and his followers in the *Galon Tat* ("the Garuda Force"). U Saw himself is often referred to as 'Galon U Saw'.

Gaung-baung. A kind of turban used by Burmese males. Part of the national dress.

ICS. The Indian Civil Service.

IP. The Imperial Police.

KNU. The Karen National Union. Set up in February 1947 by Saw Ba U Gyi to protect the interests of the Karen ethnic minority. Resorted to armed struggle in January 1949 and is still fighting the central government in Rangoon.

Lakh. Hindi (and Urdu) for 100,000.

Longyi. A Burmese sarong worn by men and women alike. *Pasoe* is the proper name for a male *longyi* and *htamein* for a woman's *longyi*.

Nat. Spirit, good or evil, in Burmese popular belief.

New Times of Burma. English-language newspaper in the 1940s and 1950s, founded and originally edited by U Tin Tut who was assassinated in 1948.

NLD. The National League for Democracy. Set up on 24 September 1988 by Aung San's daughter, Aung San Suu Kyi, and some former army officers, among them Gen. Tin U. Won a landslide victory in the May 1990 election: it captured 392 out of 485 contested seats—but the assembly was never convened.

PVO. The People's Volunteer Organisation. (*pyithu yebaw tathpwe* in Burmese; hence the abbreviation PYT, which is sometimes seen even in English texts). Set up on 1 December 1945 as an association for wartime veterans but, in effect, it became a militia force loyal to Aung San before his assassination on 19 July 1947. It later split into two factions: a "Yellow Band" PVO led by Bohmu Aung, one of the Thirty Comrades who was close to the Socialist Party, and the much more left-leaning "White Band" PVO led by another of the Thirty Comrades, Bo La Yaung, and Bo Po Kun, also a veteran of World War Two. The "White Band" PVO went underground on 28 July 1948. Bo La Yaung surrendered in the early 1950s; Bo Po Kun continued fighting under the new banner the People's Comrade Party until August 1958 when he also surrendered. Several PCP leaders later entered legal politics and some became members of the Burma Socialist Programme Party (BSPP) after the 1962 military takeover.

Myanma Alin. "The New Light of Burma". One of Burma's leading Burmese-language newspapers during the democratic period.

Myochit. Patriot (literally "Love of Country"). U Saw's political organisation was called the *Myochit* Party. It disintegrated after his arrest in July 1947.

Sangha. (Pali.) Assembly or order of monks.

Sawbwa. (In Shan: *saohpa*, "Lord of the Sky".) Prince; title used by the hereditary rulers of the thirty or so Shan states until 1959.

Saya. "Teacher" used in a broad sense (to show respect for learned people).

Sayadaw. Royal title for abbot of Buddhist monastery.

SLORC. The State Law and Order Restoration Council. The official name for the junta that assumed power in Burma on 18 September 1988.

Sun. U Saw's newspaper.

Tat. Literally "force". There were many *tats*, or private armies, in Burma in the late 1940s, among them U Saw's *Galon Tat*.

Tatmadaw. "The Armed Forces"; name used even in English texts for Burma's army (*kyee tatmadaw*), navy (*yay tatmadaw*) and air force (*lay tatmadaw*).

Thoke-thin-ye. A Burmese expression meaning to remove rivals by complete annihilation.

Working People's Daily. Mouthpiece for the Burma Socialist Programme Party until September 1988. Since then Burma's only legally permitted daily newspaper. Controlled by the military. Now renamed "*Myanma Alin*" (in Burmese), and "The New Light of Myanmar" (in English) (not to be confused with the original *Myanma Alin*).

Notes on Sources

Chapter 1
This chapter is based on numerous conversations with my father, Maj.-Gen. Tun Hla Oung, my father-in-law, Justice Thaung Sein, and my uncle, U Shwe Baw (who miraculously escaped being assassinated on 19 July 1947), and on talks with persons who lived in Rangoon during that period, plus my own experiences. I have compared their accounts with that given in *A Trial in Burma: The Assassination of Aung San* by Dr. Maung Maung (The Hague: Martinus Nijhoff, 1962). Details about Thakin Nu's appointment as Prime Minister come from his autobiography *Saturday's Son* (Bombay: Bharatiya Vidya Bhavan, 1976), pp. 133–134.

Chapter 2
This chapter is based on books written by Burmese as well as foreign authors: Dr. Htin Aung, U Nu, Dr. Ba Maw, Brig. Maung Maung, Izumiya Tatsuro, Hugh Tinker and others who are listed in the bibliography (see ditto). Thakin Hla Pe's (Bo Let Ya) quote comes from Dr. Maung Maung, *Aung San of Burma* (The Hague: Martinus Nijhoff, 1962), p. 47.

Chapter 3
Details about the trial (and quote) come from *A Trial in Burma: The Assassination of Aung San* by Maung Maung (The Hague: Martinus Nijhoff, 1962), and as told to me by my father and father-in-law. Burmese-language sources include local newspapers such as *Thuriya* (The Sun), *Myanma Alin* (New Light of Burma), *Hanthawaddy*, *Yangon* and *Economic* and other dailies which were published at the time, plus more recent magazines and journals, including *Forward* and the *Working People's Daily* (both in English).

Chapter 4
Anthony Stonor sent a written account of his encounter with Thakin Than Tun to me in 1989. However, the incident was never reported in the media at the time and no one has been able to identify the other Burmese man who that day reportedly accompanied Thakin Than Tun to the Officers' Club in Rangoon.

Notes on Sources

The government statement of 25 July 1947 is an official press release which was carried by several local newspapers at the time. The quote from the *Rangoon Guide Daily* was included in a telegram from Sir Hubert Rance to the Earl of Listowel (dated Rangoon 28 July 1947, 1725 hrs; IOR: M/4/2714). Details about Bingley and the other Englishmen were related to me by my father, Tun Hla Oung. See also *Burma: the Struggle for Independence 1944–1948* by Hugh Tinker (London: Her Majesty's Stationery Office, 1984), pp. 731–737.

Chapter 5

For a comprehensive background to political events in Burma at this time (including the murder of Tin Tut), see *The Union of Burma: a Study of the First Years of Independence* (London: Oxford University Press, 1967) by Hugh Tinker. The story about Colin Tooke was told by Anthony Stonor and is supported by Michael Busk (the police officer who arrested David Vivian). C. Henry Young is still alive and lives near Three Pagodas Pass on the Thai-Burma border. The Karen theory appeared in the April 1986 issue of the *KNU Bulletin*. Dr. Kyin Ho's 16-page booklet, *Bogyoke Aung San hne Myanma Arzanimya Lokkyan Hmugyi Atwinyemya* ("The Inside Story of the Assassination of General Aung San and Burma's Martyrs"), was published by himself in Fort Lauderdale, Florida, in 1992.

Chapter 6

The references to the Kempetai are based on private conversations with former MIS officers who told me about its nefarious activities. Dr. Maung Maung's *Burma and General Ne Win* (Bombay: Asia Publishing House, 1969) is a sycophantic attempt at white-washing the old dictator, but it nevertheless contains some useful material. Details about the killing of Sai Myee were provided by his brothers, Tzang and Harn Yawnghwe, who now live in Canada. *Time* magazine published a graphic account of the massacre of the South Korean leaders in late 1983. Bertil Lintner's *Outrage: Burma's Struggle for Democracy* (Bangkok: White Lotus, 1990) gives a comprehensive account of the worst excesses of the Ne Win regime, and inspiration has also come from his numerous reports and analyses in the *Far Eastern Economic Review*.

Index

Index

Index